GAMES TEAMS PLAY

DYNAMIC ACTIVITIES FOR TAPPING WORK TEAM POTENTIAL

LESLIE BENDALY

McGRAW-HILL RYERSON LIMITED

Toronto / Montréal / New York / Auckland / Bogotá / Caracas / Lisbon / London
Madrid / Mexico / Milan / New Delhi / San Juan / Singapore / Sydney / Tokyo

McGraw-Hill Ryerson Limited
300 Water Street
Whitby, Ontario L1N 9B6

2 3 4 5 6 7 8 9 0 MP 5 4 3 2 1 0 8 7

Canadian Cataloguing in Publication Data

Bendaly, Leslie
    Games teams play

ISBN 0-07-552718-9 (pb) — ISBN 0-07-552719-7 (looseleaf)

1. Work groups. 2. Personnel management. I. Title

HD66.B45 1996	658.3'128	C96-930758-6
HD66.B45 1996a	658.3'128	C96-930781-0

Publisher: **Joan Homewood**
Editor: **Erin Moore**
Production Coordinator: **Sharon Hudson**
Cover Design: **Steve Eby**
Interior Design/Composition: **McGraphics Desktop Publishing**
Editorial Services: **Allyson May**

This book was composed in Palatino, Optima and Zapf Dingbats typefaces, using Adobe PageMaker 6.0.

Printed and bound in Canada by Maracle Press using acid-free and recycled paper.

This book is dedicated to all of the teams who are committed to fully tapping their potential.

Contents

Part II Workouts

PART I

Introduction

CHAPTER
1

A FACILITATOR'S GUIDE TO TURNING WORK GROUPS INTO TEAMS

INTRODUCTION

Facilitating the metamorphosis of work groups into teams is one of, if not the most important role in today's organization.

If you are raising your eyebrows even slightly, consider this.

We know that:

- In order to thrive in the new economy an organization must constantly and expertly introduce and manage change.
- In today's organizations change must be introduced and managed by teams.
- If teams don't work, change doesn't work.
- If change doesn't work, the organization doesn't survive.

Turning work groups into teams is essential to an organization's survival, let alone its ability to thrive.

Frequently the label of team is arbitrarily handed to any group of people who come together to get a job done. As a result, teamwork is often maligned as it becomes equated with the wheel spinning, conflict, and mediocre or poor outcomes of groups calling themselves teams. As those of you reading this are aware, teams don't just happen, they are developed. Groups should have to earn the title of "team" by demonstrating the definition of a team.

A TEAM IS A HIGHLY EFFECTIVE, COHESIVE GROUP OF INDIVIDUALS WHO WORK TOGETHER WITH COMMITMENT TO REACH A COMMON GOAL.

Put most simply, a team is a healthy, fit group.

Games Teams Play presents activities, or workouts, that help groups to develop the level of fitness required to become a team. They also help teams that are already fit to maintain that fitness and to become even better. Team fitness requires ongoing assessment and the commitment to change that brings about growth. These team development activities presented in this book act as a catalyst and provide the framework for team growth.

HOW TO USE THIS BOOK

Each workout can stand alone; however, *Games Teams Play* also provides a team development system, to assist the leader or facilitator to introduce an ongoing development process. At the center of the team development system is the Team Fitness Test (Handout 2.2), a diagnostic tool that may be used to assess a team's strength with respect to the five elements critical to team effectiveness: Shared Leadership, Group Work Skills, Climate, Cohesiveness, and Team Members' Contribution. A separate chapter is devoted to each element and consists of a collection of workouts to strengthen that element.

Several activities can be woven together to create a team development workshop. The workouts are designed to provide whatever support you need to create and facilitate team development sessions that will bring about exceptional change, whether you are an experienced professional or a novice facilitator. I have included a wide variety of activities. Each triggers important discussion and results in commitments to action for change and growth.

SELECTING WORKOUTS

Option 1

Select one workout for use in a short (1 hour to 1.5 hour) meeting or to supplement other team development material. In order to facilitate your selection you might consider the Team Fitness Elements and choose the one that you believe the team would benefit most from strengthening. Turn to the section that focuses on that element and select the workout that best matches the team's personality. See "Workout Selection Index According to Fitness Elements", page 31. Alternatively, refer to the "Workout

Selection Index According to Skills and Development Areas", page 33, which identifies the teamwork skill(s) developed by each activity.

Option 2

Use *Games Teams Play* to design a team development workshop. Invite team members to complete the Team Fitness Test. The data collected will indicate which elements most require strengthening. Turn to the sections that focus on these elements and select workouts that best match the team's needs and personality.

Structure: The Key to Facilitation Success

Highly effective team development sessions flow with such ease and flexibility that to the participant or casual observer they appear quite unstructured. Underlying that free-flowing process is a well-planned structure used with intuitive flexibility.

Each workout is designed to provide that structure, as well as guidelines to ensure the requisite flexibility. We must ask you to add the intuition!

Each workout is structured as follows:

Elements Strengthened. As previously discussed, the Team Fitness Test allows you to assess a team's strength in several elements critical to high performance teamwork. Workouts are collected in chapters headed by the element which they are designed to best strengthen. However, many workouts strengthen more than one element. All of the elements strengthened are indicated at the top of each activity.

Objectives. This section provides more specific information as to the benefits to be reaped by the team.

Time Required. Very often the time required depends on the importance of issues raised by an activity, the level of discussion, the developmental needs of the team, the size of the group, and so on. While approximate times are provided, the facilitator's own sense of the time required is most relevant.

Materials Required. Many workouts require no materials at all. Those materials that are required are indicated here.

Background. This section provides the facilitator with information that will increase his or her understanding of the workout and its importance. The information can also be used to enrich the facilitator's introduction of the activity.

Steps. Instructions are provided with a level of detail that will support the experienced or novice facilitator.

Tips. Under this heading I present approaches that I have found to enhance the workout.

Discussion Questions. Each workout ends with a discussion that examines the observations and learning that took place through the workout. If the workout is an experiential activity, the discussion section acts as the debriefing. The discussion ensures, to as great extent as possible, that the workout leads to learning and that the lessons acquired are applied to bring about substantive change. Questions are provided to support the facilitator in leading the discussion, and common responses are offered where the discussion is quite universal and it is felt that some information about how other teams have responded would help facilitators in their preparation. Some workouts lead to discussion that is very unique to the team. When this is the case common responses are not offered.

Outcome. What the team will have accomplished (will go away with) at the end of the workout. This will usually include **commitments to action** or **working agreements**.

Notes. Space is left for personal notes, so that all of your information may be gathered in one place for easy reference.

Additional Support. Each workout includes as much support material as possible, including workout guidelines, participant's notes, worksheets, copy for overhead transparencies, and game pieces.

Icons

Icons indicate when various tools and materials are to be used:

handout overhead

These symbols appear in the left margin of the text.

Level of Difficulty

The level of complexity is determined by the expected sensitivity of the issues that the workout may spark, and consequently the skill required in facilitating the process.

Activities marked with ✪ are quick and easy to use, with no extensive experience required on the part of the facilitator. Most require 15 to 30 minutes although some are longer.

Those to which ✪ ✪ are attached are of moderate complexity and usually take longer.

Activities assigned ✪ ✪ ✪ are more sophisticated, usually more involved, and therefore longer workouts. They usually work at a higher level of team development.

Both ✪ ✪ and ✪ ✪ ✪ workouts provide sufficient guidelines for a facilitator of any level of experience to take a team through the steps. In selecting the workouts the facilitator must consider the type of discussion he or she would anticipate arising from the workout, and his or her comfort in effectively facilitating that discussion.

TIPS FOR FACILITATING A POWERFUL TEAM DEVELOPMENT PROCESS

This section is primarily for those who are relatively new to the role of facilitator, but more seasoned professionals may choose to skim it to refresh their memories.

Creating a Positive Process

A positive group process is one in which dialogue is open and leads to productive outcomes. Participants leave a positive process feeling good about themselves, their team mates, the process they have experienced, and the outcomes, at least to the extent that they are willing to support them.

A positive process is dependent to a great extent on the quality of the dialogue. Participants must be able to raise issues that may be sensitive, and to give and receive feedback.

The facilitator cannot single-handedly ensure the quality of the dialogue. Team members must take ownership for the way in which they communicate. This happens when team members stop to think about the behaviors required for a positive process and make agreements to demonstrate those behaviors.

Workshop Agreements

A set of agreements for open communication clarifies what members need from one another in order to be open and the requirements for a "safe" environment. It also gives members "permission" to be open. By referring to the agreements as needed throughout the workshop, the facilitator helps the group to use its agreements to create a positive process.

You might develop the agreements by using the "Developing Feedback Agreements" workout found on page 123.

If, in the process, the following agreements are not identified by the group, the facilitator might recommend that they be adopted.

We agree:

That all feedback will be given with a positive intent.
In other words, members will not use the forum to dump on other members or vent their feelings in a non-constructive manner. Any opinions voiced will be put forward for the purpose of making things better, perhaps by clarifying a situation or helping to solve a problem.

That feedback or input will present facts not perceptions.
Input is not internalized and used if the receiver is feeling defensive. Nothing arouses a defensive response more quickly than a judgmental statement. "You don't support the team" is a judgmental statement based on perception which is almost guaranteed to trigger a defensive response and block any potential dialogue. "You don't attend team meetings" is a comment based on fact and not as likely to trigger emotion.

The amount of time spent on developing working agreements will depend on:

- The group's climate (level of trust and consequently openness). This may be determined by the Team Fitness Test (Handout 2.2).

- The sensitivity of the issues to be discussed.

- The length of the team development session.

Too often groups assume it is the facilitator's job to make the group process work. Developing workshop agreements emphasizes that the success of the group process is a shared responsibility.

If you are prepared to spend between 20 and 40 minutes on the development of the agreements, you might want to use the "Technique for Developing and Organizing Ideas" that follows.

The Technique for Developing and Organizing Ideas

The Technique for Developing and Organizing Ideas is a useful tool that can be used to facilitate discussions in which you wish to:

- Increase the number of ideas

- Ensure equal participation

- Achieve group closure/outcomes

TECHNIQUE FOR DEVELOPING AND ORGANIZING IDEAS

Step 1. **Clarification of the objective.**

Step 2. **Silent generation of ideas.**

Step 3. **Round robin feedback of ideas.**

Step 4. **Group clarification and discussion of each recorded idea.**

Step 5. **Agreement on priority ideas.**

Step 6. **Recap.**

Step 7. **Commitment to action.**

This Technique, or a variation of it, is a mainstay of many effective facilitators.

Techniques similar to this are often referred to as brainstorming techniques. I suggest, however, that when facilitating processes that require a high degree of creativity, that the technique used should be somewhat less structured.

The Technique for Developing and Organizing Ideas increases participation and therefore the number of ideas generated, protects ideas and participants by preventing judgmental responses, and provides a structure that helps to keep the group on track and allows it to achieve its objective in an efficient manner.

Step 1. *Clarification of the objective.*

Even if the objective of the discussion appears obvious, check for clarification. When discussion gets off track, it is often because participants have different perceptions of what the group is trying to achieve. They may have a common understanding about **what** is being discussed (the topic) but different perceptions as to **why** it is being discussed (the objective). Post the objective. If the discussion is off track, bring the group's attention back to the objective.

Step 2. *Silent generation of ideas.*

This is the step most often ignored, and in my experience it is the most powerful one.

Consider the difference between the two following scenarios and what will ensue. The group's objective is to improve the effectiveness of its meetings.

Facilitator: "You have suggested that you believe your meetings are not as effective as they might be. What do you believe should be done differently in your meetings?"

or

Facilitator: "You have suggested that you believe your meetings are not as effective as they might be. Please jot down on the paper in front of you two or three ideas for improving your meetings' effectiveness."

In the first scenario, people are simply asked for their ideas. When this happens, the few people who love to participate and think comfortably out loud quickly begin speaking. Others may not have yet collected their thoughts, may be more hesitant to speak, or may not care.

As soon as anyone speaks the process begins to be limited because:

1. Everyone is influenced to some degree by others' thoughts; and

2. The norm is to begin talking about the ideas presented, what is liked or disliked, or perhaps how the ideas might be built on. But frequently the number of subsequent original ideas is limited.

The second scenario, in which the facilitator asks participants to jot down their ideas, has many advantages:

- Without stating it the facilitator sends the message that everyone is expected to contribute.

- Everyone quickly gets into the process. (They begin thinking.)

- Team members who tend to work best independently and quietly have an opportunity to collect their ideas in a manner that works well for them.

- Each member is doing original thinking, not influenced by others' thoughts.

- The number of suggestions generated is greatly increased.

This step does not take long, only three or four minutes, but the benefits are enormous.

Step 3. *Round robin feedback of ideas.*

This refers to the common practice of going around the group and inviting each person to contribute his or her idea(s).

Ideas are recorded on a board, flipchart, etc.

Suggestions:
Explain before you initiate this step that you would like one idea from each person and that you will continue to go around until all ideas are out. (If time is limited you may ask for the top one or two.)

and

That you ask that the idea not be discussed until all ideas are out.

This will prevent judgmental responses, either positive or negative, from influencing the formation of ideas not yet tabled. This will also prevent the idea generating process from getting sidetracked.

If the issue is sensitive and the group is not sufficiently developed to be open with one another, you may wish to collect the ideas and present them yourself.

Another variation is to have individuals write their ideas on pieces of paper large enough to allow them to be read from a distance, and posting them.

Step 4. *Discussion of each idea.*

Establish an agreed upon time for discussion based on the number of ideas generated.

Step 5. *Agreement on priority ideas.*

At this point, participants are moving into a decision-making mode.

Support for ideas selected is greatly dependent on the level of comfort with the decision-making process. Therefore it is important to facilitate agreement on how the group will prioritize the ideas or select the "best" idea. This could include developing a list of decision-making criteria which will clearly define what the decision will be based upon. For groups that have not worked with criteria before and which may have difficulty identifying criteria, asking this simple question can help: "What does the best idea/solution/decision look like?" Responses usually come quickly, e.g., "It is one that costs the least, or is easily implemented", etc.

Step 6. *Recap.*

Recapping ensures understanding and consensus.

Step 7. *Commitment to action.*

Identify who is responsible for taking ideas to the next step and when.

Honing Your Intuition

Highly effective facilitators have well developed intuition. They are able to quickly get a "feel" for a group and instinctively know what will work and what won't. Even before meeting the group, the facilitator's intuition is at work in the planning process.

Some facilitators are more intuitive by nature, making it perhaps somewhat easier for them to facilitate a process that leads to remarkable outcomes. They are, as we say, "naturals".

Everyone, however, can increase his or her level of intuition and consequently his or her success as a facilitator. In addition to natural abilities, intuition increases with experience, preparation, and being tuned into the group.

Before a facilitator has extensive experience to rely on, he or she can greatly enhance intuitive ability, the ability to sense what is "right", through preparation.

Preparation, however, means far more than gathering information about a group, selecting activities, etc. It means visualizing what each piece of the workshop will look and feel like and most importantly how the group will respond. Facilitators who demonstrate high levels of intuition and responsiveness in team development sessions have played the workshop over step by step in their mind's eye. They have programmed into the scene the knowledge they have of the group (its size, type of work performed, work with their minds, work with their hands, etc., etc.), what the room and set up might look like, and the various options for workshop activities. As they "see" themselves leading the group through a particular activity they picture the likely response to the activity and can usually sense quite quickly what will work and what won't.

Preparation makes it much easier to tune into the group during the workshop. If the facilitator is prepared, he or she can focus on the group rather than the details of what comes next.

Balancing Flexibility and Structure

Flexibility is the alter ego of structure. Each balances the other. The facilitator who focuses on structure to the exclusion of flexibility tends towards rigidity and drives rather than facilitates the process.

On the other hand, the facilitator who values flexibility to the exclusion of structure creates a limp process that focuses on keeping everyone happy rather than achieving productive, consensual outcomes. Much discussion and wheel spinning but few outcomes, or outcomes that are not supported, are the result.

When something is not working well the flexible facilitator quickly and smoothly changes direction, perhaps simply uses a process check such as: "I don't think this is working. Am I right?"

Highly skilled facilitators can change direction and redesign or create activities on the spot. If you don't think you are there yet, take along some backup activities and discussion questions.

Clarifying the Team Development Process

Much of the team development process parallels a problem-solving and continuous improvement process. Team development facilitators in the recent past were commonly called team builders. No facilitator or leader can build the team; the team must build itself. Essential to the team's ability to do this is a well facilitated team development process in which *the team pauses for reflection and self-examination, identifies opportunities for improvement, and commits to acting on those opportunities.*

Figure 1.1
The Team Development Process

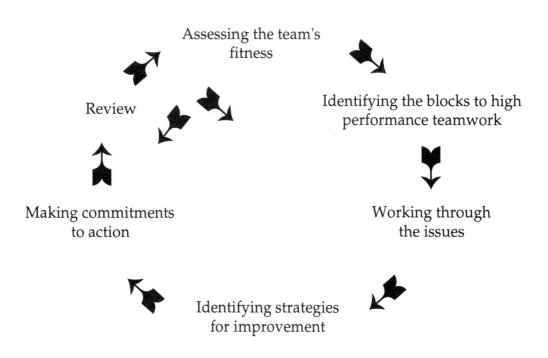

Assessing the team's
fitness

Identifying the blocks to high
performance teamwork

Review

Working through
the issues

Making commitments
to action

Identifying strategies
for improvement

Team development works best when the process is ongoing and teamwork behaviors become a habit.

Setting Team Development Goals

Team development, like any other initiative, is unlikely to be successful unless it is clear what success looks like. Being a better team is not specific enough. What does being a better team look like? How will the team know when it has become "better"? If you opt not to use the Team Fitness Test, these are questions to be asked early on in a team development process. The answers should form team development goals and be monitored regularly.

THE TEAM FITNESS TEST

INTRODUCTION

The Team Fitness Test is not a magic wand, but it may be the closest thing to one that a team development facilitator can have in his or her repertoire of tools. Teams that use the Team Fitness Test effectively experience a greatly accelerated team development process.

In order for a group to become a team or for a team to become even better than it is, the goals to be achieved must be clearly understood. Team members usually have ideas as to what could be better in their team. Few, however, have specific knowledge of what is required for high performance teamwork. Therefore, even when a team is consciously trying to improve, critical aspects that may be blocking team performance are often overlooked. The Team Fitness Test ensures that team members understand what creates high performance teamwork and focuses the team's attention on the areas that will bring the greatest return.

Team development happens best when a system that supports an ongoing development process is in place. The results of the Team Fitness Test prioritize development needs and provide a benchmark. The system is a simple one involving the following steps:

1. Examining Team Fitness Test results.

2. Identifying and celebrating strengths.

3. Identifying opportunities for growth.

4. Acting on the opportunities for growth.

Teams beginning the development process use the Fitness Test every two to three months to monitor progress. As the team reaches levels of high performance, they continue to use the Fitness Test to help maintain their performance level and to continue to enhance it. Some apply the test every six months, others once a year if their life-line extends that far.

One of the greatest benefits of the Fitness Test is that it quickly turns the ownership for the development of the group over to the team. When the facilitator shares the data, it is important to emphasize that this is the team's view of itself, its strengths and opportunities: "Here is how you see your team."

When examining the responses and discussing opportunities for growth, once again, the team members' responsibility is obvious. Asking "What do you believe you can do to strengthen this element?" will lead us to specific team agreements and commitments to action which must be followed up and reinforced regularly. Each of the workouts that the facilitator may select to support the strengthening of a specific element also leads the group to team agreements or commitments to action, i.e., more effective teamwork.

USING THE TEAM FITNESS TEST

Pre-Workshop Steps

1. Distribute the Team Fitness Test (Handout 2.2) and the Team Fitness Scoring Sheet (Handout 2.3) to each team member. Ask them to record their responses on the "Team Fitness Scoring Sheet", and to forward it to you, keeping a copy for themselves. Ask them to bring this copy to the workshop.

2. Assure team members that their responses are confidential and that names are not required.

   Tip: To ensure confidentiality, ask respondents to fax or send responses directly to you.

3. Compile the data. For each element add all scores and divide by the number of responses. Record team scores and ranking on the Interpretation Sheet (Handout 2.4).

4. Note the range of scores (i.e., lowest and highest) for each element as indicated. This is particularly important if responses differ greatly or if one or two responses are considerably higher or lower than the rest and so affect the average.

5. Examine the lowest scores and look for statements that were consistently given a low rating. From this information select appropriate workouts.

6. Plan how the team can most productively discuss the results.

In the Workshop

1. Distribute copies of the Team Fitness Elements (Handout 2.1).

2. Display Overhead 2.1 and discuss the Team Fitness Elements.

3. Distribute copies of the Team Fitness Interpretation Sheet (Handout 2.4).

4. Ask participants to complete columns headed "Your Score" and "Your Ranking" for each of the five indicators, by referring to their own copy of the "Team Fitness Scoring Sheet".

5. Interpret the results from the Team Fitness Test. Teams seldom just happen, they are developed. Therefore, unless a team has made a conscious effort to develop, it is unlikely to produce scores of 18+. If a team has not been focusing on its development and produces high scores (an uncommon scenario) the facilitator must challenge the team to ensure that their self-examination has been honest.

6. Discuss the results from the Team Fitness Test.

   Recognize the team's strengths based on the elements that received the highest scores.

   For each element that offers opportunities for improvement, ask the following two questions:

   • Why do you think the [   ] element is relatively weak?

   • What can you, the team members, do to strengthen this element?

7. Identify points of agreement.

8. Recap points of agreement and commitments to action.

Outcome

The benefits to be gained from taking the Team Fitness Test include acquiring an understanding of team strengths and opportunities for improvement, increased ownership on the part of team members for team development, and team commitments to action to increase team effectiveness.

TEAM FITNESS ELEMENTS

Shared Leadership

Group Work Skills

Climate

Cohesiveness

Team Members' Contribution

Team Fitness Test

Rate each of the statements as it applies to your team using the following rating scale:

This statement <u>definitely</u> applies to our team.	4
This statement applies to our team <u>most of the time</u>.	3
This statement is <u>occasionally</u> true for our team.	2
This statement <u>does not describe</u> our team at all.	1

Enter the score you believe appropriate for each statement beside the statement number on the Scoring Sheet.

1. Each team member has an equal voice.

2. Members make team meetings a priority.

3. Team members know they can depend on one another.

4. Our mandate, goals, and objectives are clear and agreed upon.

5. Team members fulfil their commitments.

6. Team members see participation as a responsibility.

7. Our meetings produce excellent outcomes.

8. There is a feeling of openness and trust in our team.

9. We have strong, agreed upon beliefs about how to achieve success.

10. Each team member demonstrates a sense of shared responsibility for the success of the team.

From *Games Teams Play*, by Leslie Bendaly. © McGraw-Hill Ryerson 1996

Team Fitness Test (cont'd)

11. Input from team members is used whenever possible.

12. We all participate fully in team meetings.

13. Team members do not allow personal priorities/agendas to hinder team effectiveness.

14. Our roles are clearly defined and accepted as defined by all team members.

15. Team members keep each other well informed.

16. We involve the right people in decisions.

17. In team meetings we stay on track and on time.

18. Team members feel free to give their honest opinions.

19. If we were each asked to list team priorities, our lists would be very similar.

20. Team members take initiative to put forth ideas and concerns.

21. Team members are kept well informed.

22. We are skilled in reaching consensus.

23. Team members respect each other.

24. When making decisions, we agree on priorities.

25. Each team member pulls his or her weight.

HANDOUT 2.2

From *Games Teams Play*, by Leslie Bendaly. © McGraw-Hill Ryerson 1996

Team Fitness Scoring Sheet

I		II		III		IV		V	
Statement	Score	Statement	Score	Statement	Score	Statement	Score	Statement	Score
1		2		3		4		5	
6		7		8		9		10	
11		12		13		14		15	
16		17		18		19		20	
21		22		23		24		35	
Total		Total		Total		Total		Total	

Team Fitness Interpretation Sheet

Column	Your Score	Your Ranking	Team Score	Team Ranking	Range of Score	Team Range	Team Fitness Element
I							Shared Leadership
II							Group Work Skills
III							Climate
IV							Cohesiveness
V							Team Members' Contribution

Your lowest score will be ranked number 1, second lowest score number 2, etc.

Workout Selection Index According to Fitness Elements

Workout Selection Index According to Fitness Elements (cont'd)

Workout Selection Index According to Skills and Development Areas

Workout		Page No.	Problem Solving and Decision Making	Meeting Effectiveness	Communication	Creativity	Team Members' Development	General Teamwork Development	Interpersonal Relations	Inter-team Relations	Conflict Management	Team Values	Focusing the Team	Measuring Success	Influencing Ability	Empowerment	Change Management
3.1	Death in the Desert	39	✓			✓											
3.2	Meeting Effectiveness Barometer	51		✓													
3.3	Creating Dialogue	57		✓	✓												
3.4	Checking Your Dialogue	69		✓	✓		✓										
3.5	Creating the Great Escape	75	✓			✓											
3.6	Learning the Balancing Act	85		✓													
3.7	Meeting for Better and for Worse	95		✓													
3.8	Who's Listening?	101	✓		✓		✓										
3.9	As I Remember	103	✓						✓	✓							
4.1	Developing Feedback Agreements	123	✓	✓	✓				✓								
4.2	Strengthening Inter-Team Relations	127			✓					✓							
4.3	The Teamwork Basics: Avoiding Communication Glitches	135			✓			✓	✓								✓
4.4	Getting Rid of Old Baggage	145			✓				✓								✓
4.5	Clarifying Expectations	147			✓				✓	✓							
4.6	I'll Bet You Didn't Know	151							✓	✓							
4.7	Fact or Fancy	153	✓						✓		✓						
4.8	Checking Your Team's Climate	155			✓				✓	✓							
4.9	Opening Communication	163			✓				✓	✓							
4.10	Proud to be a Member	167							✓	✓							
4.11	Taking Ownership for Conflict Management	169	✓		✓				✓		✓						
4.12	Changing Hats	175			✓			✓		✓							
5.1	Name that Team	181				✓		✓					✓				
5.2	Strengthening Team Connections	183								✓							
5.3	Selling the Team	189				✓		✓							✓		
5.4	Building a Cathedral	197						✓					✓	✓			
5.5	Developing Customer-Focused Goals	199				✓		✓						✓	✓		
5.6	Values Check	203						✓						✓	✓		
5.7	Focusing the Team I	209						✓							✓		

Workout Selection Index According to Skills and Development Areas (cont'd)

PART II

Workouts

CHAPTER
3

Team Fitness Element:
GROUP WORK SKILLS

GROUP WORK SKILLS

A team's ability to work effectively in a meeting setting is critical to its effectiveness outside of the meeting. If the best decisions are not made, or if true consensus is not achieved, a team cannot function at its best.

The Group Work Skills element reflects the quality of decision making and problem solving, consensus reaching, meeting management, and facilitation. Synergistic and productive meetings are reflected in the energy and success displayed in a team's day-to-day operations.

WORKOUTS

	Title	Level of Difficulty	Time Required	Page Number
3.1	Death in the Desert	✪	25 mins.	39
3.2	Meeting Effectiveness Barometer	✪	20 mins.+	51
3.3	Creating Dialogue	✪ ✪	1 hour+	57
3.4	Checking Your Dialogue	✪	15 mins.	69
3.5	Creating the Great Escape	✪ ✪	1 hour	75
3.6	Learning the Balancing Act	✪ ✪ ✪	45 mins.+	85
3.7	Meeting for Better and for Worse	✪	45 mins.+	95
3.8	Who's Listening?	✪	10 mins.	101
3.9	As I Remember	✪	50 mins.	103

3.1 DEATH IN THE DESERT ✪

Objectives

To strengthen a team's problem-solving ability by increasing team members' knowledge of the pitfalls that problem-solving groups most commonly slip into.

Time Required: 25 minutes

Background

Teams frequently get bogged down in problem-solving sessions or end up with less than the "best" solutions. This workout highlights some of the common pitfalls. In particular, it emphasizes how frequently groups make assumptions and how severely assumptions handicap the problem-solving process.

Materials Required

Provided: Overheads (2), Handouts (2)

Steps

1. If the team has eight or more members, ask participants to form groups of four to six.

2. Explain that you are going to give the group(s) a problem to solve—a riddle. The solution will be given to one team member in each group and the group(s) must find the solution by asking that person questions that can be answered with "yes" or "no".

3. Take the designated team members aside and give them the riddle and the answer. Explain that they do not have to remember the riddle as you will give it to the whole group.

Riddle: *A man was found dead in the desert. Near him was a package. If he had opened the package he would not have died. What was in the package?*

Answer: *A parachute.*

4. Display the riddle where everyone can see it (Overhead 3.1.1), for the duration of the game.

5. Ask anyone who recognizes the riddle to act as observer in his or her group.

   If there is more than one group:

   • Ask that when a group reaches the solution, it keeps it to itselves but have members wave their arms to indicate their success.

   • You may either call the game once one group has the solution, providing there has been sufficient time (five minutes plus) for everyone to have given the riddle a good effort.

   or

   • Set an allotted time within which they must come up with the solution—approximately seven minutes.

6. Once the riddle has been solved, give each group a copy of the "Death in the Desert" participant's worksheet (Handout 3.1.1). Ask participants to take five minutes to identify two behaviors/actions that helped them to solve the problem or move toward the solution and two that slowed them down or prevented them from reaching the solution.

Responses might look like this:

Aiding Behaviors
- Listening

- Building on ideas

- Lateral thinking

- Clarifying information

- Analyzing the problem carefully

Hindering Behaviors
- Not listening

- Jumping from one idea to another without building

- Lack of lateral thinking

- Making assumptions—e.g., the desert caused his death

- Not recognizing the importance of particular aspects of a problem—e.g., in the riddle, the word "opened"

7. Ask groups to share their observations.

Discussion Questions
1) How can we transfer this learning to workplace problem solving?

Look for commonalities and present the Problem-Solving Pitfalls (Overhead 3.1.2).

Note: Participants will usually have identified these. The most powerful messages here are:

(i) The tendency to make assumptions is frequently counterproductive. Most will assume the death is somehow linked to the desert. Early questions will usually be "was it water?", or "was it a snake bite kit?"

(ii) Personal perceptions or interpretation can hinder communication. Different people will have had different ideas as to what a package might be. Some expect it to be a small box, others visualize a huge carton or even a back pack.

2) Does your team ever slip into these pitfalls when trying to solve a problem?

3) How can you prevent your team from slipping into one of these pitfalls?

Common response: "Be more aware of or monitor our process and speak up if we are slipping."

Distribute a copy of "Problem-Solving Pitfalls" (Handout 3.1.2) and suggest that it might be used as a checklist to help monitor the effectiveness of problem-solving sessions.

Outcome
Increased understanding of the requirements for effective problem solving.

A commitment to strengthen the team's problem-solving ability.

✔ **Group Work Skills**

A man was found dead in the desert.

Near him was a package. If he had opened the package he would not have died. What was in the package?

PROBLEM-SOLVING PITFALLS

The following often impede a problem-solving process:

◆ **making assumptions**

◆ **differing perceptions, lack of clarity re terms and definitions (e.g., package)**

◆ **not listening (preoccupied with own idea/opinion)**

◆ **lack of lateral (creative) thinking**

From *Games Teams Play*, by Leslie Bendaly. © McGraw-Hill Ryerson 1996

Death in the Desert

PARTICIPANT'S WORKSHEET — GROUP

As a group: Consider your problem-solving process. List at least two aiding behaviors that helped you solve the riddle or get on the right track and two hindering behaviors that slowed you down or prevented you from reaching the solution.

Aiding Behaviors	**Hindering Behaviors**

From *Games Teams Play*, by Leslie Bendaly. © McGraw-Hill Ryerson 1996

Problem-Solving Pitfalls

PARTICIPANT'S NOTES

The following often impede a problem-solving process:

◆ making assumptions

◆ differing perceptions, lack of clarity re terms and definitions (e.g., package)

◆ not listening (preoccupied with own idea/opinion)

◆ lack of lateral (creative) thinking

3.2 MEETING EFFECTIVENESS BAROMETER ✪

Objectives

To increase meeting effectiveness.

Time Required: 20 minutes+

Background

Meeting effectiveness requires an understanding of what makes meetings work and regular assessment to ensure this requirement is met.

The "Meeting Effectiveness Barometer" (Handout 3.2.1) highlights the requirements for making a meeting work. Its use keeps those requirements in front of team members and assesses the team's meeting effectiveness.

Note: This can be used quickly at the end of a meeting if meetings are already relatively effective. Alternatively, in discussion, the facilitator could ask the group to focus on the **one** area that offers the greatest opportunity for improvement. This activity could be also used as a 1.0–1.5 hour long workshop activity.

Materials Required

Provided: Handout

Steps

1. Set aside time at the end of a meeting to use the Meeting Effectiveness Barometer.

2. Distribute copies of the participant's worksheet headed "Meeting Effectiveness Barometer" (Handout 3.2.1).

3. Ask each member to complete the Barometer individually.

4. Share responses from team members for each requirement. Ensure that members provide evidence for their rating, particularly if the rating is high or low.

5. Provide a recap of the comments; e.g., "From your comments it appears that you feel that the team clarified objectives very well, and generally did a good job of clarifying understanding. The requirements that you feel most in need of attention are staying on track and ensuring full participation."

Discussion Question

What do you suggest team members do to help ensure that the group improves the area that was identified as needing work during the next meeting?

Pose this question for each of the requirements that most deserve attention.

Possible responses:
"We need to:

-   Keep the objective in front of us.

-   Put time limits on each discussion item.

-   Remind one another that we are off track.

-   Make sure we always assign a facilitator or discussion leader."

Make the following recommendations:

(i)   That the list of agreements be reviewed at the beginning of the team's next meeting.

(ii) That there be a check at the end of the meeting as to whether the agreements were lived up to during the meeting.

(iii) That the team check its progress by periodically using the Meeting Effectiveness Barometer.

Outcome

Shared responsibility for meeting effectiveness.

More effective meetings.

Meeting Effectiveness Barometer

PARTICIPANT'S WORKSHEET

Consider the effectiveness of your meeting by rating each of the following requirements.

In your meeting did the team:

	Not well		Very well		
	1	2	3	4	Evidence
◆ Clarify objectives?					
◆ Stay on track?					
◆ Ensure full participation?					
◆ Ensure all points were understood by everyone?					
◆ Bring each item to closure/make commitments to action?					
◆ Recap outcomes?					

From *Games Teams Play*, by Leslie Bendaly. © McGraw-Hill Ryerson 1996

3.3 CREATING DIALOGUE ✪ ✪

Elements Strengthened:
Group Work Skills,
Cohesiveness, and Climate

Your Notes

Objectives

To develop a better understanding of the difference between dialogue and discussion.

To assess the team's present use of dialogue.

To increase the team's use of dialogue.

Time Required: 1 hour+

Materials Required

Provided: Overheads (2), Handouts (2)

Background

Dialogue is essential to effective problem solving and consensus reaching and to creating an environment of trust. *Groups* rely on discussion, *high performance teams* use dialogue with ease. In *The Fifth Discipline*,[1] Senge suggests that when team members engage in dialogue they enter into a genuine "thinking together". Discussion, in contrast, consists of competition.

In discussion we come from closed positions. We have firm opinions and may have already made up our minds on the issue. We make statements[!!!]. More telling than probing for information takes place. We expect others to prove to us that they are right.

---

[1] Peter Senge *The Fifth Discipline* (New York: Doubleday/Currency, 1990).

In dialogue we accept the responsibility of trying to understand others' perspectives. We are open and welcome the other person's point of view. Rather than seeing ourselves as responsible for influencing others to take a particular course, we believe that we are responsible for contributing to the body of knowledge that is being built through the dialogue, and for understanding all contributions to that body of knowledge. We recognize that ultimately the influencing force should be that fully understood body of knowledge.

In dialogue members are looking for the *best* solution not *their* solution. There is a good deal of probing for more information and understanding. "Can you explain why you feel that way?" or "I don't think I get what you are saying. Could you put it another way?" are commonly asked questions.

Dialogue requires that we:

- set aside preconceived ideas or assumptions

    and

- probe for information and understanding.

Assumptions that block dialogue are highly varied. Examples include:

- "Why bother? Nothing will change."
- "He's already made up his mind."
- "They have all the power."
- "They aren't open to ideas from us."
- "I know where she's coming from."

Once teams have identified assumptions, they recognize that assumptions are at work all of the time — although we are often not even consciously aware of making assumptions.

They also recognize the degree to which assumptions block communication effectiveness.

Once options and/or different perspectives are openly explored and understood through dialogue, the high performance team moves to a discussion mode to come to closure.

Steps

1. If dialogue versus discussion is a new concept for the team, share some of the information presented under "Background", above.

2. Use Overhead 3.3.1 as the focus for group discussion.

Ask the team to what extent this definition of dialogue is reflected in the way it works?

Note: Ask participants to substantiate their responses with specific examples.

3. Discuss the requirements for dialogue. Use Overhead 3.3.2.

4. Break the group into subgroups if numbers allow.

5. Distribute copies of "Assessing Team Dialogue" (Workouts I (Handout 3.3.1) and/or II (Handout 3.3.2)) and briefly review them.

Note: You are provided with two Team Workouts. You may use one or both depending on need and the time available.

6. Ask groups to complete the workout.

7. Invite groups to share their output and look for commonalities.

Discussion Questions

1) From the perspectives we have just shared, what conclusions can we draw about dialogue in this team?

2) What does the team need to focus on or do in order to enhance dialogue within the team?

Check for consensus and commitment to follow through on the above.

Tip: During the discussion observe the quality of discussion. Are people engaged in dialogue? Ask the team for its opinion.

If the response is yes, ask for evidence. If the response is no, ask what the group needs to be doing differently.

Outcome

An understanding of how to recognize when dialogue is taking place.

An understanding of the team's present communication style.

Commitments to action for enhancing dialogue.

Games Teams Play   Creating Dialogue
                            ✔ **Group Work Skills**
                            ✔ Cohesiveness
                            ✔ Climate

DIALOGUE

Dialogue is a very open free flow of information for which all participants take responsibility.

Dialogue requires that participants:

- ### set aside preconceived ideas or assumptions

- ### probe for information and understanding.

Team Workout I:
Assessing Team Dialogue

WORKOUT GUIDELINES — GROUP

Preconceived Ideas

Allotted time: 25 minutes

1. Appoint a group discussion leader.

2. Develop a list of possible preconceived ideas or assumptions that may block dialogue in this team.

3. Select two preconceived ideas that you believe to be the most powerful dialogue blockers. E.g., management never listens. Others will never change. My ideas will be criticized. I am right.

4. Develop recommendations for removing these preconceived ideas or for preventing them from blocking team dialogue.

5. Be prepared to share your ideas with the larger group.

Assumptions	Recommendations for Action

HANDOUT 3.3.1

From *Games Teams Play*, by Leslie Bendaly. © McGraw-Hill Ryerson 1996

Team Workout II: Assessing Team Dialogue

WORKOUT GUIDELINES — GROUP

Probing for Understanding

Allotted time: 20 minutes

1. Appoint a discussion leader.

2. Consider the following. The outcome of dialogue is true understanding. When dialogue occurs each team member leaves the meeting knowing that he or she has been understood and with complete understanding of other team members' points of view. When this is the case, probing for understanding has usually taken place.

3. Discuss:

   ◆ "Do we always leave meetings feeling we have been understood and knowing that we fully understand other's perspectives?"

   ◆ "Do we probe for understanding well?" (Probing is asking questions to bring about clearer understanding.) Substantiate your answer by using an example of a team meeting in which understanding was or wasn't evident.

4. If the consensus in your group is that your team does not enhance dialogue by probing for understanding develop a list of recommendations for rectifying this problem.

Recommendations

_____

_____

_____

HANDOUT 3.3.2

3.4 CHECKING YOUR DIALOGUE ✪

Element Strengthened:
Group Work Skills

Objectives

To check whether the team is using practices that enhance dialogue.

To develop team practices that will enhance dialogue.

Your Notes

Time Required: 15 minutes

Background

See Background notes for "Creating Dialogue", page 57.

This activity may be used with teams that have already used one of the previous dialogue workshops.

This activity should be used during a regular team meeting. Its use during any team meeting can provide useful information; however, the most dramatic results are achieved when it is used during one that has sensitive items on its agenda.

Materials Required

Provided: Handout

Steps

1. If the concept of dialogue is new to team members, set aside some time to introduce it at the beginning of the meeting. Use Overheads 3.3.1 and 3.3.2 from the "Creating Dialogue" workout.

   Set aside at least 15 minutes at the end of the meeting for discussion.

2. Explain that one means of measuring whether a group regularly engages in dialogue is to check how often probing questions are asked. Probing questions indicate that the participants are taking responsibility for understanding others' points of view. Such questions might include:

   • Could you explain it again?

   • Can you tell us more?

   • Can you give some examples of why you feel that way?

3. Ask for a volunteer to observe the dialogue during the meeting and note the presence or absence of probing. Give the observer a copy of the "Checking Team Dialogue" sheet (Handout 3.4.1). Another option is to introduce an observer from outside the team, if the team is comfortable with this.

4. After items on the regular agenda have been dealt with ask the observer for his or her comments.

5. Invite team members' responses to these observations.

6. If the observer's, the team's, and your own perception is that the team probed effectively throughout the meeting, congratulate the team. *Note:* This is not the most common outcome. Most groups do not probe well.

   If it has been recognized that the team missed opportunities to enhance dialogue and understanding with better probing, lead the following brief discussion.

Discussion Question

Considering these observations, what can the team do to enhance dialogue through more effective probing?

Check for consensus and commitment among the team.

Outcome

An increased understanding of the expectation that members take personal responsibility for fully understanding others' points of view.

An increased awareness of the importance of asking probing questions to achieve understanding.

A commitment to enhancing team dialogue through more effective probing for understanding.

Your Notes

Checking Team Dialogue

OBSERVER'S WORKSHEET

Instructions

Probing for understanding is essential to dialogue. Please take the role of observer during this meeting and assess whether team members probe effectively.

Jot down examples of probing that lead to increased understanding.

Also look for instances when opportunities for probing were missed. For example, someone's point of view was not completely understood and questions that might have helped clarify the situation were not asked.

Examples of Probing

_____

_____

_____

_____

_____

Examples of Missed Opportunities

_____

_____

_____

_____

_____

HANDOUT 3.4.1

_____

From *Games Teams Play*, by Leslie Bendaly. © McGraw-Hill Ryerson 1996

3.5 CREATING THE GREAT ESCAPE ✪ ✪

Objectives

To test the team's creativity.

To examine the team's effectiveness in using and building on ideas.

To have fun.

Time Required: 1 hour

Background

When what worked yesterday no longer works and teams are facing challenges never before experienced, creative problem solving becomes elevated above a "nice to have" skill.

Creative team thinking tends to be rare unless the team is blessed with highly creative team members or is challenged to think about the effectiveness of its problem-solving processes.

Team creativity is often stifled by too few ideas being produced or ideas being lost and not capitalized on.

This workout puts the team into a situation where the need for creativity is evident and challenges the team to assess its creative problem-solving abilities, particularly its ability to develop and build on ideas.

Materials Required

Provided: Handouts (4)

Steps

1. Break the group into teams of four to seven members.

2. Distribute "The Great Escape Workout" instruction sheet (Handout 3.5.1) and briefly review it.

3. Assign an observer for each team and give each observer a copy of "Assessing the Creative Process" (Handout 3.5.2), several copies of the "Tapping Ideas" sheet (Handout 3.5.3), and review their instructions.

4. Allow 20 minutes for the completion of the Great Escape.

5. Give observers an additional five minutes to complete their comments.

6. Ask each team to describe the escape they have devised. Look for opportunities to congratulate teams on originality and humor.

7. Distribute a copy of the workout guidelines (Handout 3.5.4) to each participant.

8. Allow approximately 20–25 minutes for the assessment process.

9. Ask each team to share at least one commitment to action.

Outcome

Greater awareness of the team's creative problem solving process, its strengths and weaknesses.

Specific commitments to enhance the team's creative problem-solving process.

The Great Escape Instructions

PARTICIPANT'S NOTES — GROUP

You are competing for the contract to write the script for a multi-million dollar action film starring the number one action hero, Spruce Gillis. You are given 20 minutes to finish writing the following scene.

The action is set in a library in a Mediterranean villa. The room is on the ground floor. There is one entrance to the room, a heavy oak door. The two windows have no glass but are covered with ornate wrought iron bars.

The hero kills the villain. But before he dies the villain manages to lock the door to the room they are in, tosses the key through a barred window, and dies laughing. Your hero soon realizes why. He spots a bomb on a timer. The timer indicates that he has four minutes until the bomb detonates.

He looks out the window and sees the key on the ground about five feet (1.5 m) below.

On the set are the following props. You may use any of these props to devise the hero's escape.

Props

Furniture:
Desk, swivel high-backed chair, sofa, lamp table, and lamp.

Other items:
Note pad, pens and pencils, books, ink, tissues, blotter, paper clips, scissors, rubber bands, scotch tape, lap top computer, bottle of scotch, two crystal glasses, small woven rug (2 ft. x 4 ft. (.6 m x 1.2 m)), newspaper, magazines, disconnected telephone, letter opener, envelopes, a bowl of gum drops, bouquet of flowers, an umbrella stand holding an umbrella and a cane.

Assessing the Creative Process

OBSERVER'S WORKSHEET

The Role of the Observer

As observer your responsibility is to:

1. Observe the aspects of the group's process that contribute to or hinder creative solutions.

2. Report back to the team on the above.

As you observe the process, refer to the sheet headed "Tapping Ideas" (Handout 3.5.3), jot down each new idea or suggestion that is put forward, and chart the response to the idea and what ultimately happens to it by circling the appropriate descriptors in column 2 (Response) and column 4 (End result). In column 2 there may be more than one response. Circle each and number them in order of response. If time allows, record the responding team member's name.

Assessment

From the observations you have made, what do you conclude about the team's effectiveness in tapping everyone's ideas?

Consider

◆ Did most members participate fully in the process?

◆ Did the team produce plenty of ideas?

◆ Was it okay to put forward "crazy ideas?"

◆ Did team members listen to one another well?

◆ Did team members build on each other's ideas, making good ideas even better?

◆ Did the team lose potentially important ideas/input?

Give examples to substantiate your impressions.

_____

_____

HANDOUT 3.5.2

Observer's Worksheet—Assessing the Creative Process (cont'd)

Other Comments:

_____

_____

_____

Reporting Back to Your Team

Present to your team:

1. A general overview of your observations.

2. Two or three examples from your "Tapping Ideas" sheets.

3. Your observations from the Assessment above.

Tapping Ideas

OBSERVER'S WORKSHEET

TAPPING IDEAS

Idea...	Response	By whom	End result
	ignored		accepted
	criticized		built on
	built on		lost
	used		
	rejected		

Presented by:

TAPPING IDEAS

Idea...	Response	By whom	End result
	ignored		accepted
	criticized		built on
	built on		lost
	used		
	rejected		

Presented by:

TAPPING IDEAS

Idea...	Response	By whom	End result
	ignored		accepted
	criticized		built on
	built on		lost
	used		
	rejected		

Presented by:

Creating the Great Escape

WORKOUT GUIDELINES — GROUP

Allotted time: 20 minutes

After your observer has shared his or her observations:

1. Discuss your observer's observations.

2. Develop a list of ways in which the team or team members can enhance the use of ideas, increase creativity, and produce better solutions.

3. Select at least three of the above ideas and state them as working agreements.

We agree that in order to increase our creativity and problem-solving ability we will:

_____

_____

_____

_____

_____

_____

_____

_____

_____

HANDOUT 3.5.4

From *Games Teams Play*, by Leslie Bendaly. © McGraw-Hill Ryerson 1996

3.6 LEARNING THE BALANCING ACT ✪ ✪ ✪

Objectives

To recognize the importance of balancing the attention the team gives to task and to team process.

To increase awareness of the team's task/process orientation.

To increase team effectiveness through maintaining optimum team task/process balance.

Time Required: 45 minutes +

Background

Task refers to what the team does; process refers to how the team works together to achieve the task. Task includes goals and objectives, decisions, problems, issues, and actions. Team process includes group interaction, dialogue, checking feelings, checking for understanding, participation, communication, brainstorming, collecting information, creativity, etc.

When the team is too highly task oriented the team process required to ensure quality outcomes is overlooked. Closure occurs too early. The best decisions will not be made and/or the support required to make them work will not be there.

When the team is too process oriented, it may lose sight of the task. Wheel spinning can become the norm; there is too little closure. Issues are not resolved or outcomes are forced because someone realizes that *something* has to be done. Results are often similar to those of the highly task-oriented group—poor quality outcomes and lack of support for those outcomes.

There is frequently more frustration, however, in the highly process-oriented group because members often recognize the wheel spinning. In the task-oriented group members often believe they are simply being very efficient.

High performance teams find the balance. They are able to move with ease between a task orientation and a process orientation.

They know when to stay tightly focused and close discussion down, and when to open things up and check for responses and feelings, look for input and feedback, etc.

Materials Required
Provided: Overhead, Handouts (2)

Steps
1. Pre-workshop

   • Video a team meeting.

   • Select a segment or segments, up to 15 minutes in length, that illustrate task-oriented behaviors and process-oriented behaviors in the team.

2. Introduce the concept of team task/process balance using the information from "Background" (above) and Overhead 3.6.1.

3. Distribute the Assessing Team Task/Process Balance worksheet (Handout 3.6.1) and the participant's notes headed "The Key to High Performance Teamwork" (Handout 3.6.2).

4. Briefly review the participant's notes and the worksheet with the participants.

5. Play the selected video segment and ask members to observe and make notes on their team's task/process balance using the worksheet.

6. Allow an additional five to ten minutes for completion of the worksheet.

7. Invite participants to share their observations and responses.

8. Recap the team's consensus on its task/process balance (Part B2 on the worksheet).

Discussion Question

What can you do to better balance your team's attention to task and attention to process?

Recap commitments to action and check for consensus.

Outcome

A list of commitments to action that will increase teamwork effectiveness by better balancing the team's attention to team task and to team process.

BALANCING TEAM TASK AND TEAM PROCESS

Task-Oriented Behaviors	*Process-Oriented Behaviors*
Focusing on WHAT	**Focusing on HOW**
Clarifying goals	**Dialoguing**
Clarifying objectives	**Attending to climate**
Making decisions	**Being facilitative**
Using an agenda	**Inviting participation and participating**
Being directive	**Encouraging discussion**
Staying on track	**Thinking creatively**
Moving discussion along	**Brainstorming**
Coming to closure	**Checking how people feel**
Making judgment calls/decisions	**Checking for understanding**
Telling	**Probing for information**
Focusing on detail	**Looking at the bigger picture**

Assessing Your Team's Task/ Process Balance

PARTICIPANT'S WORKSHEET

Take a few minutes to review Handout 3.6.2, "The Key To High Performance Teamwork — Achieving the Task/Process Balance". Use it for reference as needed while watching the video.

While watching the video:

Part A

1. List comments/behaviors that are task oriented:

    Team Member   Comment/Interaction

    _____

    _____

2. List comments/behaviors that are process oriented:

    Team Member   Comment/Interaction

    _____

    _____

Part B

1. You have viewed a segment from one team meeting. Do you believe that what you have seen reflects the team task/process balance that is most often demonstrated in your team? Provide examples to support your response.

    _____

    _____

2. How would you rate your team's task/process balance? Circle the number that you believe best reflects its balance.

Task Oriented   Process Oriented

1   2   3   4   5   6   7   8   9   10

HANDOUT 3.6.1

From *Games Teams Play*, by Leslie Bendaly. © McGraw-Hill Ryerson 1996

The Key to High Performance Teamwork — Achieving the Task/Process Balance

PARTICIPANT'S NOTES

Task refers to what the team does and process refers to how the objectives are achieved. Task includes goals and objectives, decision making, problems, issues, and actions. Process includes group interaction, dialogue, communication, attending to climate, gathering information, and creative thinking.

When the team is too highly task oriented the process required to ensure quality outcomes is overlooked. Closure occurs too early. The best decisions will not be made and/or the support required to make them work will not be there.

When the team is too process oriented wheel spinning can become the norm; there is too little closure. Issues are not resolved or outcomes are forced because someone realizes that *something* has to be done. Results are often similar to those of the highly task-oriented group — poor quality outcomes and lack of support for those outcomes.

Balancing Task and Process

Task-Oriented Behaviors	*Process-Oriented Behaviors*
Focusing on WHAT	Focusing on HOW
Clarifying goals	Dialoguing
Clarifying objectives	Attending to climate

HANDOUT 3.6.2

From *Games Teams Play*, by Leslie Bendaly. © McGraw-Hill Ryerson 1996

Balancing Task and Process (cont'd)

Task-Oriented Behaviors	*Process-Oriented Behaviors*
Making decisions	Being facilitative
Using an agenda	Inviting participation and participating
Being directive	Encouraging discussion
Staying on track	Thinking creatively
Moving discussion along	Brainstorming
Coming to closure	Checking how people feel
Making judgment calls/ decisions	Checking for understanding
Telling	Probing for information
Focusing on detail	Looking at the bigger picture

3.7 MEETING FOR BETTER AND FOR WORSE ✪

Objectives
To increase meeting effectiveness.

Time Required: 45 minutes+

Background
Most teams need to commit considerable time to meetings. Meetings have a bad name in many organizations because the time spent in them is often seen as non-productive time.

Meeting effectiveness can be increased quickly. This workout requires team members to consider positive meeting practices, to decide on the degree to which their meetings demonstrate those practices, and to develop working agreements that will increase their meeting effectiveness.

Materials Required
Provided: Handouts (2)

Steps
1. Distribute the "Meeting for Better and for Worse" worksheet (Handout 3.7.1).

2. You may:

   • ask members to complete the worksheet individually (allow approximately ten minutes)

   or

   • break the team into small work groups to discuss and complete the worksheet (allow approximately 15 to 20 minutes).

3. Review responses to the worksheet. Identify commonalities and discuss any differences.

4. From the discussion identify possible working agreements and record on overhead or flip chart. Check for consensus.

   Tip: Limit agreements to six or seven. A longer list is quickly forgotten.

   Examples of possible working agreements:

   — We agree not to shoot down other's ideas.

   — We agree to stay on track.

   — We agree to come to meetings prepared.

5. Distribute copies of "Working Agreements for Effective Meetings" (Handout 3.7.2) and have each member copy the agreements.

   Tip: Some teams like to develop more formal contracts and sign one another's copies.

   Note: If working agreements are to be effective they must be pulled out regularly to assess the degree to which the team is living up to those agreements.

Outcome
A set of working agreements that will increase meeting effectiveness.

Meeting For Better and For Worse

PARTICIPANT'S WORKSHEET

Part I

High performance teams have highly productive meetings. Meetings increase in effectiveness when team members recognize their meeting strengths and weaknesses and commit to improvement.

Please identify your team's meeting strengths and weaknesses by **circling the behaviors listed below that describe your team most of the time**. If working in a group, attempt to achieve consensus on each point.

The following are our team's meeting strengths:

◆ We are clear about the purpose of our meetings.

◆ We receive agendas in sufficient time to prepare for the meeting.

◆ Members come to the meetings prepared.

◆ Our meeting objectives are clarified at the beginning of the meeting.

◆ Meetings start and end on time.

◆ Team members make meetings a priority.

◆ Our discussions stay on track.

◆ Everyone participates.

◆ We listen to one another.

◆ If team members have a concern, they raise it.

◆ If team members have an idea, they put it forward.

◆ We respond honestly to one another.

Meeting For Better and For Worse (cont'd)

◆ Agenda items deserve the team's time (they are sufficiently important to be on the agenda and/or require most member's attention).

◆ Team members demonstrate flexibility in discussions.

◆ We check for understanding as needed.

◆ We check for consensus when decisions are made.

◆ We recap decisions and action items at the end of meetings.

Part II

Examine the descriptors you did not circle and select up to five that you believe, if developed in your team, would bring about the greatest increase in meeting effectiveness.

_____

_____

_____

_____

_____

_____

_____

_____

_____

_____

_____

Working Agreements for
Effective Meetings

_____
name of team

We agree that in order to increase our meeting effectiveness we will:

◆ _____

_____

◆ _____

_____

◆ _____

_____

◆ _____

_____

◆ _____

_____

◆ _____

_____

◆ _____

_____

_____
team member

HANDOUT 3.7.2

3.8 WHO'S LISTENING? ✪

Objectives

To remind participants of the importance of listening for detail, particularly when problem solving.

Time Required: 10 minutes

Background

This activity can be used as a quick and energizing illustration of the fact that people often don't listen well. The following instructions apply particularly to problem solving and demonstrate how easy it is to get immersed in detail and miss critical points.

Materials Required

None

Steps

1. Ask participants not to use pencils to solve the following riddle, which you will present orally. (Don't hand it out in written form.)

> You are a bus driver. At the first stop 12 people get on. At the next stop 3 get off and 5 get on. At the third stop 1 gets off and 6 get on. At the fourth stop 5 get off and 8 get on. At the fifth stop 9 get off and 3 get on. At the sixth stop 3 get off and 7 get on. What is the name of the bus driver?
>
> **Answer:** Your name.

Note: Most participants get so involved in the arithmetic that they forget the opening line of the riddle or don't really hear it to begin with.

Discussion Questions

1) Why did most people not know the answer?

Common Responses:
We got sidetracked by the numbers.

We didn't really listen at the beginning.

We made assumptions about what the problem was.

2) What lessons from this activity can you apply to your team problem solving?

Recap points made and if possible, translate them into specific commitments to action.

Outcome
Greater awareness of the importance of listening for detail, particularly when problem solving.

3.9 AS I REMEMBER ✪

Objectives

To provide an opportunity to identify factors that contribute to teamwork effectiveness.

To strengthen team relationships through working together on a "fun" activity.

To have fun.

Time Required: 50 minutes

Background

"As I Remember" is a "fun" activity that energizes a group and also illustrates the importance of working agreements.

Materials Required

Provided: Handouts (2), Symbols

Other: Envelope for each group, large sheet of paper (possibly from flipchart) on which to stick symbols, adhesive

Steps

1. Pre-workshop: Copy, cut out, and fix symbols in a random pattern on a piece of paper approximately the size of a sheet of flipchart paper.

   Tip: To increase the level of difficulty of the game do not place symbols in straight rows.

2. Explain that you will be showing team members a sheet covered with a collection of symbols and their job will be to work as a team to duplicate it.

3. Divide the group into teams. Each team should ideally consist of six or more members, although smaller groups can work.

4. Distribute to each team:

  • an envelope containing a copy of each symbol

  • a piece of newsprint on which to organize the symbols

  • a set of rules (Handout 3.9.1)

5. Review the rules and allow teams five to seven minutes to look over their package of symbols and to get organized.

6. Lead the teams through the game by following the Game Rules (Handout 3.9.1).

7. Post the sheet of symbols and have each team compare their results with the original.

8. Declare the winner.

9. Distribute the "As I Remember" debriefing sheet (Handout 3.9.2). Allow teams ten minutes to discuss the points on the sheet.

Discussion Questions

1) What did you identify as the factors that most contributed to your team's success in completing this task?

Common responses:
Organization
Trusting one another's ability
Working agreements
Leadership

2) Is each of these factors strong in your team's day-to-day activities? (Ask participants to give examples to support their responses.)

3) Is there anything your team should be doing differently?

Develop comments into commitments to action as appropriate. Recap any commitments to action and check for consensus.

Outcome

Heightened awareness of factors that contribute to effective teamwork.

Strengthened team relationships.

As I Remember

PARTICIPANT'S NOTES — GROUP

Game Rules

Objective: To duplicate the master sheet as closely as possible and lose the least points.

1. Everyone views the master sheet for five seconds.

2. Each team selects one team member who will view one-half of the sheet for ten seconds.

3. The teams have approximately five minutes to work on their sheets.

4. Each team selects another team member who will view the second half of the sheet for ten seconds.

5. The teams have approximately five minutes to work on their sheets.

6. Teams may purchase additional viewings of the sheet for one point per viewing. An additional viewing consists of one team member seeing one-quarter of the sheet for ten seconds. The team selects the quarter they wish to see.

Scoring

All teams start with zero points and try to stay as close to zero as possible.

Teams lose one point for each symbol that is out of place.

Teams lose one point for each additional look at the sheet after the first three free looks.

As I Remember

PARTICIPANT'S WORKSHEET — GROUP

Debriefing

Allotted time: 10 minutes

Consider how your team worked together in the "As I Remember" game and respond to the following:

1. What factors do you believe contributed to your success in the game?

   _____

   _____

   _____

2. What prevented you from being as successful as you might have been in the game?

   _____

   _____

   _____

3. If starting over again, what would you do differently?

   _____

   _____

   _____

HANDOUT 3.9.2

From *Games Teams Play*, by Leslie Bendaly. © McGraw-Hill Ryerson 1996

WORKOUT 3.9: As I Remember Symbols

WORKOUT 3.9: As I Remember Symbols

From *Games Teams Play*, by Leslie Bendaly. © McGraw-Hill Ryerson 1996

WORKOUT 3.9: As I Remember Symbols

WORKOUT 3.9: As I Remember Symbols

From *Games Teams Play*, by Leslie Bendaly. © McGraw-Hill Ryerson 1996

WORKOUT 3.9: As I Remember Symbols

CHAPTER
4

Team Fitness Element:
CLIMATE

CLIMATE

Climate refers generally to how members feel about the way the team functions, including their level of comfort with team norms of behavior. If the climate is not positive, honesty and openness are lacking and team members may not fully trust one another. The communication process requires attention.

WORKOUTS

4.1 DEVELOPING FEEDBACK AGREEMENTS ✪ ✪

Elements Strengthened:
Climate and Group Work Skills

Your Notes

Objectives

To develop team members' awareness of the importance of feedback in creating high performance.

To develop members' ability to give and receive feedback.

To increase the effectiveness of team decision making and problem solving by promoting open communication.

Time Required: 1–1.5 hours

Background

No longer can a team just "get by". It must be better than average; it must continually function at peak performance. Peak performance is reached only when team members feel free to question and challenge one another's ideas and actions, to give one another suggestions, and to grow from the input.

Highly effective teams have systems in place that help them manage essential team practices, such as giving and receiving feedback. Systems include agreements as to how team members will work together. These agreements are reviewed regularly. In this workout, team members develop those agreements.

Materials Required
Provided: Handout

Steps

1. Distribute the "Giving and Receiving Feedback" workout guidelines (Handout 4.1.1).

2. Ask participants to work in groups of four or more to complete the group activity.

3. Ask groups to share their lists of "Requirements for Feedback".

4. Look for commonalities and develop a team list of feedback agreements (four or five).

    Examples of common feedback agreements include:

    We agree to:

    Deal with facts, not perceptions.

    Give only feedback that is well intended.

    Listen to the feedback before developing arguments or excuses.

5. Check for consensus on the list of agreements.

6. Ask the team to decide and commit to how the agreements will be used.

    Some options:

    (i) Appoint a feedback coach and ask him or her to keep an eye on the agreements during meetings and provide team members with feedback when appropriate, during or at the end of the meeting.

    (ii) Periodically review the agreements at the end of a meeting to check whether team members are living up to the agreements.

Note: If giving and receiving feedback is a serious challenge for the team, agreements should be reviewed at every meeting.

Outcome

A set of feedback agreements.

More effective giving and receiving of feedback.

Giving and Receiving Feedback

WORKOUT GUIDELINES — GROUP

No longer can a team just "get by". It must be better than average; it must continually function at peak performance. Peak performance is reached only when team members feel free to question and challenge one another's ideas and actions, to give one another suggestions, and to grow from the input.

Group Activity

Allotted time: 25 minutes

1. Consider the requirements for effective feedback by individually completing the following statements. You may write as many statements as you wish.

   I would be more comfortable giving honest feedback in our team if . . .

   _____

   _____

   I would be more comfortable receiving feedback if . . .

   _____

   _____

2. Record each member's responses on your flipchart under the heading "Requirements for Feedback".

3. Discuss each statement and combine those that are similar.

4. Identify the statements that you all agree to be important.

5. Be prepared to share them with the larger group.

HANDOUT 4.1.1

4.2 STRENGTHENING INTER-TEAM RELATIONS ✪ ✪ ✪

Objectives
To strengthen relations between interdependent teams.

Time Required: 2–3 hours (Two meetings for each team – 1 to 1.5 hours per meeting)

Background
This workout is designed to strengthen relations between teams that depend to some degree on one another to get the job done. It challenges the teams to examine what they need from one another and the strengths and weaknesses in their relationship, and leads members to develop commitments to action for change that will strengthen the relationship.

Materials Required
Provided: Handouts (2)

Steps
Part A
Each team meets separately to reflect on its relationship with the other team, as described in the following steps.

1. Distribute the "Strengthening Inter-Team Relations" worksheet (Handout 4.2.1).

2. Brainstorm to identify why it is important that the two teams work together effectively. Ask participants to recap the agreed upon points on their worksheet under "Benefits of Our Relationship".

3. You may ask members to complete the rest of the worksheet individually or

break into groups of three or more members. Allow ten minutes for completion if members are working individually, and at least 20 minutes if working in groups.

4. Invite members to share their responses.

5. Discuss and identify commonalities.

6. Organize points to be shared with the other team using the sheet headed "Our Perspective" (Handout 4.2.2).

7. Identify:
   (i) A team spokesperson who will take the lead in presenting the team's perspective to the other team.

   (ii) Someone to prepare a copy of the "Our Perspective" sheet to give to the other team at the two-team meeting.

Part B
Two-team meeting

1. Ask each team to share its points from the "Our Perspective" sheet section by section, i.e., each team presents the benefits, and then what we appreciate about you, etc.

2. Lead teams to agreement on key points under "What we need to do differently" and "What we would appreciate you doing differently".

   Note: Frequently what one team lists under "What we need to do differently" is on the other team's "What we would appreciate you doing differently" list.

3. Recap commitments to action made by each team and check for consensus.

4. Ask team members to select and agree on a follow-up system to ensure that

the headway made through this process will not be lost.

Outcome

Better understanding of one another's perspectives.

A stronger inter-team relationship.

More effective outcome from joint team-work efforts.

Strengthening Inter-Team Relations

PARTICIPANT'S WORKSHEET

Respond to the following with the team with whom you are building relationships in mind.

Benefits of our relationship:

_____

_____

_____

_____

_____

_____

The strengths the team brings to our relationship (skills, positive behaviors, etc.):

_____

_____

_____

_____

_____

_____

HANDOUT 4.2.1

Strengthening Inter-Team Relations — Participant's Worksheet (cont'd)

What we could do differently to strengthen the relationship:

_____

_____

_____

_____

_____

What the other team could do that would strengthen our relationship:

_____

_____

_____

_____

_____

HANDOUT 4.2.1

From *Games Teams Play,* by Leslie Bendaly. © McGraw-Hill Ryerson 1996

Our Perspective

PARTICIPANT'S NOTES — GROUP

Benefits of our relationship:

_____

_____

_____

Strengths you bring to our relationship:

_____

_____

_____

What we believe we need to do differently to strengthen our relationship:

_____

_____

_____

What we would appreciate you doing differently:

_____

_____

_____

HANDOUT 4.2.2

4.3 THE TEAMWORK BASICS: AVOIDING COMMUN- ICATION GLITCHES ✪ ✪

Objectives

To improve the team's communication effectiveness.

Time Required: 50 minutes +

Background

The most essential ingredient in an effective team is a basic one; we are all aware of it and yet this ingredient is the one most often missing: effective communication.

It should be simple enough; we all learned to communicate when we were babies. Yet communication creates some of the greatest challenges. Most dysfunctional teams cite it as number one on their list of opportunities for improvement. Healthy teams usually recognize that they could become even stronger if communication were enhanced.

As communication is improved, relationships are enhanced and the foundation of the team is strengthened.

If a team is to build its foundation, it must self-examine and make commitments to action for improvement. This workout helps team members to examine "teamwork affirmations" and "teamwork glitches".

Teamwork affirmations are instances when positive interactions/communications strengthen team performance.

Teamwork glitches are instances when interactions/communications are not positive or a communications opportunity is ignored.

Identifying Teamwork Affirmations and Glitches

The figure below shows how affirmations and glitches can be visually identified.

The circle represents the team. Team members' names are plotted around the circle. Each team member is asked to consider his or her interactions with other team members over a specific period of time — perhaps two weeks.

A team member's personal teamwork affirmations and glitches profile might look like this.

Figure 4.1

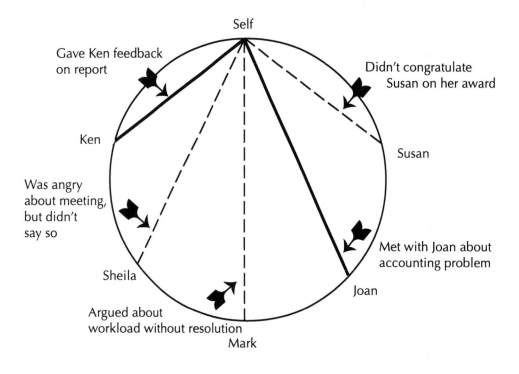

———— Teamwork Affirmations

— — — Teamwork Glitches

Materials Required
Provided: Overheads (2), Handout

Steps

1. Introduce this activity as an opportunity to strengthen the team's foundation, its communication effectiveness.

2. Define affirmations and glitches, using Overhead 4.3.1.

3. Distribute the participant's worksheet, the Affirmations and Glitches Personal Map (Handout 4.3.1).

4. Take the group through an example (Overhead 4.3.2).

5. Give participants five to ten minutes to complete their Personal Maps.

6. Interpret the Maps.
   Explain to team members that:

   — — — — —

   Glitches are hairline cracks in the team's foundation. If these are not attended to and/or if there is a large number of cracks, the foundation is weakened.

   Each affirmation acts to support the team's foundation. If teamwork affirmations are not plentiful, this also indicates possible weakness.

7. Ask participants to share their personal maps, or at least one glitch or affirmation, including what they have recognized about their interactions and specific commitments to action for enhanced communication.

   Tip: Provide participants with personal maps on an overhead transparency and transparency markers. They can then use the overhead to share and explain their maps.

Your Notes

Discussion Questions

1) What have you recognized about your interactions?

2) What do team members need to do differently?

Ask each team member to make one personal commitment to action for strengthening communication with other team members.

Outcome

A better understanding of the team's communication patterns.

A commitment to specific actions to strengthen the team's communication effectiveness.

An increased sense of personal responsibility for teamwork effectiveness.

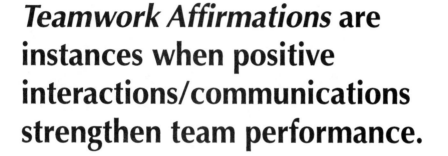

***Teamwork Affirmations* are instances when positive interactions/communications strengthen team performance.**

***Teamwork Glitches* are instances when interactions/ communications are not positive or a communication opportunity is ignored.**

OVERHEAD 4.3.1

From *Games Teams Play*, by Leslie Bendaly. © McGraw-Hill Ryerson 1996

Games Teams Play Avoiding Communication Glitches
   ✔ **Climate**
   ✔ **Cohesiveness**
   ✔ **Team Members' Contribution**

TEAMWORK
AFFIRMATIONS & GLITCHES

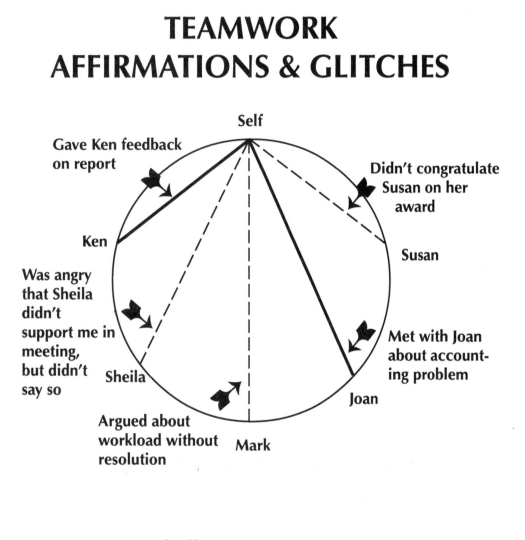

——————— **Teamwork Affirmations**
– – – – **Teamwork Glitches**

From *Games Teams Play*, by Leslie Bendaly. © McGraw-Hill Ryerson 1996

Teamwork Affirmations & Glitches

PARTICIPANT'S WORKSHEET

Your Personal Map

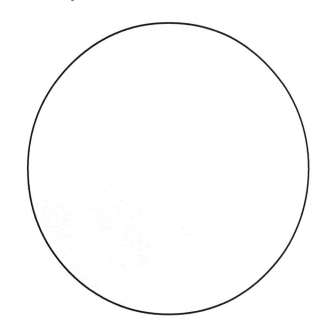

——————— Teamwork affirmations
— — — Teamwork glitches

Teamwork affirmations are instances when positive interactions/ communications strengthen team performance.

Teamwork glitches are instances when interactions/communications are not positive or a communication opportunity is ignored.

HANDOUT 4.3.1

Your Notes

4.4 GETTING RID OF OLD BAGGAGE ✪ ✪

Objectives
To assist a team in making a "fresh start" when old issues and assumptions may be holding it back.

Time Required: 45 minutes +

Background
Team development is often impeded by old issues that have not been resolved. They have been pushed underground. Although it may be officially ignored, "old baggage" can be a powerful block to teamwork effectiveness. Bringing it to the surface, acknowledging it, and agreeing to move forward greatly lessens its power.

Materials Required
A cardboard box or other receptacle labelled "OLD BAGGAGE".

Sheets of paper (at least 8 1/2" x 11" (215 mm x 279 mm) in size) for each participant. They should be large enough to have sufficient weight when crumpled into a ball to be tossed into the OLD BAGGAGE box from the participants' seats.

A pen or pencil for each participant

Steps
1. Ask team members to:

    Think of an old issue or belief that is no longer valid, but is being kept alive and so bogging the team down (e.g., management never listens),

    and

Crumple the paper on which they have written the "old baggage" and toss it into a box or other container that you have placed at the front of the room or in the centre of the group.

2. Pull the "old baggage" items out one at a time and discuss them.

Discussion Questions

1) Do most of you see this as "old baggage"?

2) How is it preventing you from moving ahead?

3) What can you do to get rid of this piece of old baggage?

Look for commonalities among the responses to the last question.

Ask for commitment to the agreed upon points.

Outcome

A list of commitments to action that members will take to remove old baggage and to move forward.

Increased understanding of one another.

4.5 CLARIFYING EXPECTATIONS ✪ ✪

Objectives
To develop a better understanding of one another's needs and to commit to making an effort to meeting these needs.

Time Required: 1 hour

Background
If morale is low or there is conflict within the team it is often because the team has not taken time to explore the needs of its individual members. Team members may be hurt or frustrated because their expectations are not met. Frequently, however, these expectations have not been articulated and others are either unaware of them or do not understand the importance the team member attaches to them. Expectations are often based on personal needs.

Clarifying expectations is a powerful activity that can quickly enhance team climate and cohesiveness.

Materials Required
None

Steps
1. Select one of the following incomplete statements to act as a thought trigger for participants.

    a) *"In order to give my best to the team I need my teammates to . . ."*

        or

    b) *"I believe we would be a more effective team if team members . . ."*

or

c) *"I am sometimes disappointed when team members . . ."*

2. Ask participants to complete the statement independently.

   Note: Expectations identified are usually basic needs that can be quite easily met by other team members.

3. Ask team members to share their statements.

   Common response (to statement a, for example):

   I need my teammates to keep me better informed; I need my teammates to be more readily available to help me out when I'm swamped and they are not as busy.

4. Discuss each of the statements, possibly using the following questions.

Discussion Questions

1) Is this a realistic expectation?

Common response:
Yes

If the response is yes,

2) Is there anything preventing anyone from living up to (name of team member)'s expectation?

Common response:
No

If no,

3) Is everyone then prepared to make a commitment to meet this need?

Usual response:
Yes

Note: If the team or any member feels that it cannot live up to a team member's need, this may lead to a recognition that a team member holds an unrealistic expectation. It may also present an opportunity for the team to look for a creative solution — what else might be done to solve this team member's concern?

Encourage follow through by asking:

4) How can you ensure that team members live up to these commitments?

Common responses:
We must each make a personal commitment to do so.

The person who has expressed a particular need must remind us if we are slipping.

Everyone must be receptive to reminders if we are not living up to a commitment.

Outcome
A clear understanding of one another's needs.

Specific commitments to meeting each other's needs to the extent possible.

4.6 I'LL BET YOU DIDN'T KNOW ✪

Your Notes

Objectives

To get to know one another.

To have fun as a team.

Time Required: 15 minutes +

Background

This activity asks team members to think of something about themselves (preferably something unusual) that other team members don't know or to invent something about themselves. Examples of personal information might be "I've travelled around the world; I have my pilot's licence; I collect black widow spiders." Each team member shares his or her piece of information with the team and the team members must decide if the information is true or false.

Materials Required

Prize if desired

Steps

1. Ask each team member to develop a personal statement starting with "I'll bet you didn't know that I . . ."

2. Invite team members to share their statements.

3. After each statement ask each team member to vote true or false. Then ask the owner of the statement to declare whether the statement was true or false.

4. Keep a tally of team members' scores. Each time a member guesses correctly he or she receives +1. Incorrect guesses are awarded -1.

5. At the end declare the winner. You may award a prize to "The Individual Who Best Knows Their Team Members" or, in a new team, to "The Most Intuitive Team Member".

Outcome

A warmer team climate.

Increased knowledge and understanding of one another as "people".

4.7 FACT OR FANCY ✪

Objectives
To increase awareness of the ease and frequency with which assumptions are made.

To increase understanding of how assumptions can be a serious block to team performance.

Your Notes

Time Required: 20 minutes

Background
This activity asks team members to describe an article and then determine which characteristics are fact and which are assumption. The leader helps participants to apply this fact vs. assumption lesson to relationships and decision making.

Materials Required
A pen (or other object)

Steps
1. Hold up a pen and ask participants to describe it. Encourage them to come up with as many characteristics as possible. Responses will likely include the color, size, who it belongs to, whether it is cheap or expensive, and the color of the ink.

2. Record the characteristics on a flipchart.

3. On a second chart or board write the headings "Fact" and "Assumption".

4. Ask participants which characteristics belong to the fact category and which to assumption.

    E.g., Fact — It is black.
    Assumption — It belongs to the facilitator.

Discussion Questions

1) What has this illustrated?

Common responses:
- It's easy to confuse fact and assumption.
- We often don't realize that we are making an assumption.

2) Can you think of any examples from work in which fact and assumption became blurred?

3) What were the outcomes when this happened?

4) What can you do to prevent assumptions from being made?

Common responses:
- When someone makes a generalized statement we have to ask them for facts to back it up.

- We have to remind ourselves not to make assumptions and to take responsibility for basing our actions and perceptions on fact.

Outcome

Heightened awareness of the negative role assumptions can play in teamwork.

An increased sense of personal and team responsibility for basing attitudes, decisions, and actions on fact.

4.8 CHECKING YOUR TEAM'S CLIMATE ✪ ✪

Objectives
To increase awareness of the level of trust and open communication within the team.

To develop commitments to strengthening the team's climate.

Time Required: 1 hour

Background
This activity provides team members with an opportunity to explore their team's climate by looking at characteristics that indicate the health of that climate. The "Checking Your Climate" questionnaire helps participants to focus their thoughts and promotes discussion.

Materials Required
Provided: Overhead, Handout

Steps

1. Distribute copies of the "Checking Your Climate" questionnaire (Handout 4.8.1) and allow approximately ten minutes for its completion.

   Tip: The questionnaire can be completed before the session. However, if climate is known to be a sensitive issue within the team, it is more effective to have team members complete it in the session where:

   • the facilitator has an opportunity to discuss climate with the group and to explain why they are being asked to spend time looking at their climate;

- there is no opportunity for misunderstanding of the motives behind this activity; and

- there is no opportunity for team members to discuss responses and influence one another's perspective.

2. Collect and compile the responses.

Tip: Use your prior knowledge of the team to determine how you will go about this step.

If climate is a sensitive issue, collect the responses and give members a ten-minute break while you compile the data.

If there is relative openness within the team participants may share their responses verbally for you to record on a flipchart or overhead. This openness may have been indicated by previous use of the Team Fitness Questionnaire. *Don't assume openness.*

Having team members personally share their ratings and observations brings the most powerful results from the activity; however, if the readiness of any team members to do so is in doubt, opt for the more cautious route of collecting, compiling, and presenting the data yourself.

3. Organize the data as presented on the overhead provided (Overhead 4.8.1).

For example, the team's data for openness might look like this:

Indicator: Openness
Individual ratings: 3, 3, 2, 3, 4, 2, 4, 2, 2
Range of ratings: 2 to 4
Average rating: 2.75

4. Use the ratings to identify which indicators require the most attention.

5. Use the data to promote discussion and the development of commitments to action.

Discussion Question

Considering the areas we have identified as most needing attention, what can you do to strengthen your team's climate?

Tip: If time allows and the team is large enough (six or more members) break into smaller groups for discussion and the development of a list of actions that would strengthen the team's climate.

Outcome

Greater sensitivity to the team's climate.

Better understanding of the factors that influence the team's climate.

Commitments to action that will strengthen the team's climate.

✔ Climate

CHECK YOUR TEAM'S CLIMATE

Indicator	Individual Ratings	Range of Ratings	Average Rating
Openness			
Support			
Sharing Success			
Dealing With Conflict			
Trust			
Team Values			

Check Your Team's Climate

INSTRUCTIONS

The following team characteristics are team climate indicators. Please rate your team candidly on the scale of 1 to 4 for each, where —

1 =   we need a lot of work in this area

and

4 =   we are very strong in this area.

In order to choose a rating for each Indicator, you may want to consider the questions listed under Thought Triggers.

Indicator	Thought Triggers	Rating			
Openness	Are team members honest and open with each other? Do people ensure that there are no hidden agendas? Do people feel free to express what they are really thinking?	1	2	3	4
Support	Do team members help each other? Are they forgiving of errors? Do they freely help others to perform more effectively? Do they present their team members positively to others.	1	2	3	4
Sharing Success	Do team members take pride in each other's successes? Are they sincerely happy for others' success? Do they look for opportunities to give each other recognition? Do they bring team members' accomplishments to the attention of others?	1	2	3	4
Dealing With Conflict	Does your team deal with small problems before they become issues? Are differences of opinion seen as normal and healthy? Are team members able to separate personalities from the issue at hand?	1	2	3	4
Trust	Do you feel that team members have the team's interest at heart? Do team members have each other's interests at heart? Can you depend on other team members to back you up? To back up the team?	1	2	3	4
Team Values	Do team members hold similar work values? Do they consistently demonstrate these values?	1	2	3	4

HANDOUT 4.8.1

4.9 OPENING COMMUNICATION ✪ ✪ ✪

Objectives
To remove barriers to open communication.

Time Required: 1–2 hours

Background
This workout is most effective if lack of open communication has been recognized by the team as an impediment to its performance. It has been rated at a high level of difficulty to facilitate because, although the concept of open communication is easily understood by most participants and the steps are straightforward, the facilitator must ensure that discussion remains productive and positive, i.e., that it focuses on issues not people. If it is possible that the team leader's actions or style are preventing open communication, the facilitator must ensure beforehand that the leader is able, with the facilitator's support, to be open to feedback.

Materials Required
Sheets of paper (at least 8 1/2" x 11" (215 mm x 279 mm)) and felt marker or crayon for each member

Steps
1. Introduce the workout by linking it to the team's needs, i.e., explain why this workout was chosen.

2. Distribute sheets of paper (at least 8 1/2" x 11" (215 mm x 279 mm) in size) and felt tip markers or crayons.

3. Ensure participants are seated far enough apart to allow them to work privately.

4. Ask participants to individually identify what they believe to be a major block to open communication in the team, to write it as briefly as possible in large letters on their sheet of paper, and fold the paper.

   Common responses:
   Fear of repercussions, being shot down, wanting to avoid conflict.

5. Post the collected responses on a board. With help from the group, organize similar points under common headings.

6. Discuss each barrier, looking for ways to remove it.

Discussion Questions

1) Some team members are concerned about . . . (fill in the identified barrier to communication). Sometimes concerns are based on perceptions and fears rather than facts and experience. What is this concern based on?

2) What can team members do to remove this barrier?

Record responses to the above question and look for consensus on one or two points. Then ask the group:

3) If everyone lives up to these commitments is it agreed that this barrier will be removed or weakened?

If the response is yes, remove all sheets from the board relating to that barrier, tear them, and discard.

Repeat these questions for each barrier. End by recapping commitments to action and checking for consensus.

Outcome

Increased understanding of the team's barriers to open communication.

Personal recognition of how one's own behaviors can create barriers to communication.

Team commitments to action for removing barriers and opening team communication.

4.10 PROUD TO BE A MEMBER ✪

Objectives
To enhance team commitment.

Time Required: 15 minutes

Background
Team commitment can be enhanced by reminding ourselves of and sharing the positive aspects of the team and why we are proud to be members of it.

Materials Required
None

Steps

1. Ask team members to individually complete the following sentence:

   Being a member of this team is important to me because . . .

   or

   I am proud to be a team member of this team because . . .

2. Share the responses.

3. Discussion of the responses may be appropriate, but is often anticlimatic. The statements can usually stand alone.

Outcome
Enhanced team commitment and experience.

4.11 TAKING OWNERSHIP FOR CONFLICT MANAGEMENT
✪ ✪

Objectives
To identify common sources of conflict.

To develop working agreements to lessen conflict.

Time Required: 1–2 hours

Background
Conflict resolution is often identified by teams as critical to performance. What teams may not recognize is that conflict prevention is even more important.

Teams can make great strides by examining a recent conflict in light of a few factors that frequently contribute to team conflict. Recognizing and examining the contributing factors frequently resolves the conflict if it is still active.

Teams usually recognize that those factors contribute not only to the specific conflict being examined but form a team behavioral pattern that can be changed. Changing the pattern prevents conflict.

Materials Required
Provided: Overhead, Handout

Steps
1. Introduce the contributing factors to conflict (Overhead 4.11.1).

2. Distribute copies of the "Conflict Contributing Factors Wheel" (Handout 4.11.1).

3. Ask participants to work in groups. If the team is larger than eight members, break into groups of four to six. Allow 30 minutes.

4. Ask groups to share their observations.

Discussion Questions

1) Which of the contributing factors do you believe are most often at play in team conflicts?

2) Considering these factors, what can you do differently that will help prevent future conflict?

Outcome

A better understanding of sources of conflict.

A set of working agreements that will lessen conflict.

Lessened conflict.

CONFLICT CONTRIBUTING FACTORS

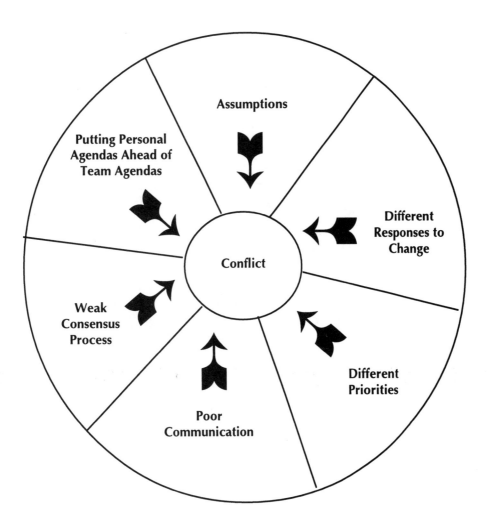

From *Games Teams Play*, by Leslie Bendaly. © McGraw-Hill Ryerson 1996

Confict Management
Contributing Factors Wheel

PARTICIPANT'S WORKSHEET — GROUP

In your group complete the wheel by:

1. Identifying a recent team conflict.

2. Identifying the contributing factors.

3. Listing any contributing factor not already indicated on the wheel in the blank segment.

4. Providing evidence and examples to support your choice of contributing factors.

Confict Management Contributing Factors Wheel (cont'd)

4.12 CHANGING HATS ✪ ✪

Your Notes

Objectives

To lessen concerns about "hidden agendas".

To increase openness between team members.

To acknowledge the various priorities team members bring to a team.

Time Required: 45 minutes +

Background

This is useful for any type of team. It has been of particular benefit to cross-functional teams whose members have concerns about the agendas and priorities that other team members bring to the team.

It can also be used early in the life of the team to acknowledge the fact that members may have different priorities based on their department's needs or their own professional needs. Acknowledging these possibly different perspectives, discussing and better understanding them makes it "O.K." to address them directly, comfortably, and productively.

Materials Required
Provided: Handout

Steps

1. Explain to the group that it is common for team members to bring different priorities and perspectives to a team. What is important is that these differences be acknowledged and understood and that if at any time a personal agenda appears to be counterproductive to the team agenda that it be discussed openly.

2. Distribute a copy of "The Hats I Wear as a Team Member" to each member (Handout 4.12.1).

3. Allow ten minutes for the completion of the sheet.

4. Ask team members to describe the different hats they wear that could affect their perspectives and priorities as well as any challenges they may face as a result of wearing the different hats.

   E.g., One member might list their hats as that of:

   • a manager of the company

   • a systems specialist

   • a member of this team

   • the chair of the Equal Opportunity Committee.

Discussion Questions

1) Do the several hats described pose any challenge to this team's ability to fulfil its mandate?

If the answer is yes,

2) What can the team do to help members manage their various hats?

or

3) What can the team do to ensure that the various priorities and perspectives brought to the team enhance rather than hinder the team's work?

Outcome

A better understanding of the various priorities, perspectives, and concerns members bring to the team.

Agreements as to how these differences can be handled openly and constructively.

The Hats I Wear as a Team Member

PARTICIPANT'S WORKSHEET

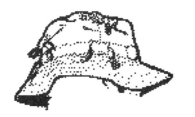

_____   _____

_____   _____

Team Fitness Element: COHESIVENESS

COHESIVENESS

Cohesiveness refers to the degree to which the group pulls together. Cohesiveness requires agreement and commitment to *what* the team is in place to achieve (mandate, goals, and objectives) as well as *how* it will achieve it (values, priorities, and procedures).

WORKOUTS

5.1 NAME THAT TEAM ✪ ✪

Your Notes

Objectives

To create or increase a sense of team identity or team spirit.

To identify or reinforce important team values.

To have fun.

Time Required: 45 minutes +

Background

High performance teams are clear about *who* they are as well as *what* they do. Many teams perform much the same tasks. What makes a team unique is *how* it approaches its tasks. Team values determine the how.

To be useful values must be appropriate to the team's mission and goals and therefore must be examined within that context.

Materials Required

None

Steps

1. Choose one of the following:

   • Post the team's mission statement if one has already been developed.

   • Post the team's goals.

   • Lead the team in the development of a "success statement" describing what success looks like to the team; e.g., "Success is increasing our market share by 20% in two years."

2. Use the Technique for Developing and Organizing Ideas (page 9) to develop a

list of four or five values that team members believe they must consistently demonstrate if they are to meet their goals or fulfil their success statement.

If the team already has a set of team values ask team members to list them.

Examples of values frequently identified as important include responsiveness, quality, commitment, teamwork.

3. Provide team members with colored markers and newsprint. Instruct participants to create a team name and/or logo that reflects the values identified.

   Note: This may be used as an introductory workout in a workshop and the teams may adopt these names for the duration of the workshop.

Outcome

A heightened awareness of key team values.

Increased commitment to consistent demonstration of team values.

Increased team spirit.

5.2 STRENGTHENING TEAM CONNECTIONS ✪ ✪

Objectives

To increase the consistency with which team members respond to other parts of the organization.

To increase team members' awareness of the importance of inter-team relations.

Time Required: 1 hour +

Background

The concepts of team work and the learning organization have emphasized that everyone and every team is part of a system. Everything we do in one way or another affects others and everything they do affects us. We are interconnected.

The effectiveness of a team's working relationship with other teams is therefore of paramount importance.

If team members are not in concert in the way they deal with other parts of the organization, the team's credibility in the organization may be affected. Getting the support required to get things done can be hampered.

This workout takes the team through a process in which it identifies its primary contact teams, examines its connections with these teams, and identifies methods for strengthening the contacts. Primary contact teams include:

- teams that this team depends on in some way in order to get the job done; and

- teams that depend on this team in some way in order to get their job done.

Note: You may add primary contact individuals.

Materials Required
Provided: Overhead, Handout
Other: Pens/pencils

Steps

1. Lead the team in developing a list of primary contact teams.

2. Plot these teams on the Primary Contacts Map (Overhead 5.2.1). You may need to add circles. Draw lines from this team to its "PC" teams using colored markers to indicate the degree of importance of the connection: red—critical; then green, and finally blue.

3. Distribute the "Strengthening Team Connections" worksheet (Handout 5.2.1).

   Note: There are two PC teams per worksheet. Distribute the number of sheets required based on number of PC teams identified

4. Ask team members to analyze the strength of the team's connection with each PC team by completing this worksheet (allow 10 to 15 minutes).

5. Compare responses and look for agreements on actions to be taken to strengthen team connections.

6. Determine first steps to be taken, by whom, and when they should be taken.

Outcome
Strengthen connections with other parts of the organization.

A more cohesive approach in dealing with other teams.

PRIMARY CONTACTS MAP

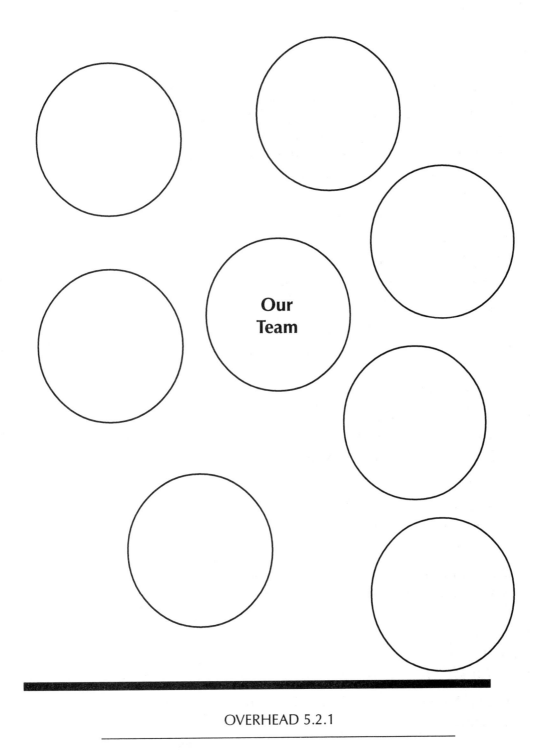

Our
Team

OVERHEAD 5.2.1

Strengthening Team Connections

PARTICIPANT'S WORKSHEET

Primary Contact Team _____

Inconsistencies in the way we presently deal or interact with this team:

_____

_____

Ways in which we can improve our response to or interaction with this team:

_____

_____

Primary Contact Team _____

Inconsistencies in the way we presently deal or interact with this team:

_____

_____

Ways in which we can improve our response to or interaction with this team:

_____

_____

HANDOUT 5.2.1

5.3 SELLING THE TEAM ✪

Objectives

To develop a clear and consistent picture of the primary service the team provides.

To help team members better communicate what they have to offer clients/customers.

To develop increased pride in the team.

To have fun.

Time Required: 1.5 hours

Background

It is generally recognized that no team can sit and wait to be discovered by clients/customers and the people who provide them with the resources to function. Teams that most effectively sell themselves are proud of what they do, and thoroughly understand the service they provide and its benefits and uniqueness.

This workout helps equip teams to better sell themselves and raise their profile.

Materials Required

Provided: Overhead, Handout

Steps

1. Identify the team's primary service, or in more general terms, reason for being.

2. Define benefits and features using Overhead 5.3.1. Example: House For Sale

   Features: 4 bedrooms
              Nanny's quarters
              Main floor family room

Benefits: Great location
Walk to public transit
Save on utilities with high tech lighting and heating systems
Entertain in spacious living room

3. Brainstorm to identify the benefits and features of the team's primary service.

4. Select the four most important features and four most important benefits.

5. Distribute copies of the "Selling Ourselves" worksheet (Handout 5.3.1).

6. Ask participants to record the primary service and the selected features and benefits in the space provided at the top of their worksheet.

7. Briefly review the group assignment instructions provided on the worksheet.

8. If the size of the team allows, break into subgroups of four or more members and if possible, move into break-out rooms. Allow 25 minutes for the assignment.

9. Invite groups to present their ads.

Discussion Questions

1) Although the ads were different, what were the consistent messages?

2) Do you communicate these messages regularly and consistently to your clients/customers?

If answer is yes, ask for examples of how this is done. If the answer is no, ask

3) What can the team do differently to ensure that a consistent and positive picture of its services is sent to clients/customers?

Recap any commitments to action and check for consensus.

Outcome

Increased pride and team spirit.

A better recognition of what, specifically, the team has to offer.

Agreed upon strategies that will help the team to more positively and consistently communicate its services to clients/customers.

✔ **Cohesiveness**

FEATURES
**are characteristics and answer
the questions who, what,
where, when and/or how.**

BENEFITS
**are how the service will meet
customers' needs and start with
action verbs such as manage,
improve, control, respond, etc.**

Selling Ourselves

PARTICIPANT'S WORKSHEET — GROUP

Our Primary Service

_____

_____

_____

_____

Benefits	Features

Group Assignment

Allotted time: 25 minutes

1. Imagine that your service can be packaged either in a can or small box.

2. Create a television ad for your service, attempting to include the key benefits and features identified. Your ad must be about 60 seconds in length.

3. Be prepared to present your ad to the larger group.

4. Have fun.

5.4 BUILDING A CATHEDRAL ✪

Your Notes

Objectives
To increase awareness of the importance, for all team members, of keeping the ultimate goal in front of them while performing day-to-day tasks.

Time Required: 20 minutes +

Background
Members of high performance teams focus on a bigger picture while carrying out day-to-day tasks. Keeping a bigger picture or vision in front of them helps members to clarify priorities and make the best decisions. It also fosters commitment and self-motivation.

This activity can be used to simply highlight the importance of team members keeping the vision in front of them, as an introduction to a team vision development, or in a refocusing session.

Materials Required
None

Steps
1. Tell the following story:

   A man was passing a work site and saw three bricklayers. He approached the first bricklayer and asked "What are you doing?" The man answered, "Making a living." He asked the second man the same question and he answered, "Laying bricks." He asked the third worker "What are you doing?" and the man responded, "Building a cathedral."

Discussion Questions

1) What would you expect to be the difference between each man's approach to his work?

2) If members of this team were asked "What are you doing?" when performing a typical task, what would the response be?

Tip: You might ask each member to write down his or her statement on a piece of paper and then share it with the team.

3) How similar are your responses?

4) If you were to respond like the man who answered "building a cathedral", what might you say? (Use this question if the responses to the second question did not indicate a sense of vision.)

Outcome

An understanding of the benefits of keeping a clear vision in front of them at all times.

Where a formal vision is already in place, a clarification of whether team members remember this vision and keep it in front of them.

or

If the team has not yet formally developed a vision, ideas as to what that vision might look like.

A recognition of the degree of consistency of the visions held by various team members.

5.5 DEVELOPING CUSTOMER-FOCUSED GOALS ✪ ✪

Objectives
To increase understanding of the benefits of setting and using customer-focused goals.

To develop customer-focused goals.

Time Required: 1.5 hours

Background
This workout illustrates the importance of clear and immediate goals to team effectiveness. Participants have the opportunity to develop customer-focused goals.

The most effective customer-focused goals are established by the team itself.

Customer-focused goals must be specific and measurable.

Examples:

- To return phone calls within two hours.

- To ensure 98% on-time delivery.

Benefits:
Customer-focused goals ensure that:

- Team members agree on priorities and place the same degree of importance on various aspects of customer service.

- Keeping an eye on goals allows teams to catch a negative trend before it becomes a problem.

- Monitoring team goals reminds team members of their successes.

- Customer-focused goals remind all team members of the importance of their individual contribution and result in an increased sense of ownership for the success of the team.

Materials Required

Game pieces, tiddly winks, or bingo markers, enough for approximately ten per participant

Steps

1. If the team has more than eight members break the team into groups of four or six members.

2. Supply each team member with approximately ten game pieces (tiddly winks or bingo markers).

3. Ask that participants shoot their game pieces across the table at random. Have them use one game piece as the lever to flip the other pieces.

   The first response will be laughter and considerable noise. Allow this to continue until there is less laughter, some people quit playing, or you hear people say "What's the objective?".

4. Then ask that each group design a game using the game pieces and play one round of the new game. This will take about ten minutes.

5. If there is more than one group, you may have them share their game ideas.

6. **Discussion Questions**

   i) What was the difference between your experience in the first half of the activity, when you were randomly shooting the game pieces, and the second half, in which you created and played a game?

Common response:
The second was more fun or more interesting.

ii) Why?

Common responses:
We had an objective/goal. We knew when we were winning. We participated in developing the goals. We had ownership for the game.

iii) How can you relate this experience to your own team?

7. Explain that teams with clear, customer-focused goals developed by the team experience the outcomes they experienced in the second half of the activity. (For more information and examples refer to "Background".)

8. Use the Technique for Developing and Organizing Ideas (page 9) or a similar method to develop a list of customer-focused goals most critical to the team's performance (five to seven maximum).

9. Develop agreements as to how the goals will be monitored.

Outcome

Customer-focused goals.

A clearer understanding of priorities.

A greater sense of pulling together.

5.6 VALUES CHECK ✪ ✪

Objectives

To assess the degree to which team members demonstrate key team values.

To increase team members' commitment to consistently demonstrating key values.

Time Required: 1–2 hours

Background

See Background from 5.1, *Name That Team* page 181.

Materials Required

Provided: Handouts (2)

Steps

1. List the team's values. If the team has not yet developed a set of team values, complete steps 1 and 2 from the *Name That Team* activity on page 181.

2. Provide each team member with a copy of the worksheets, "Demonstrating Team Values" (Handout 5.6.1) and "Team Commitments to Action" (Handout 5.6.2).

3. Ask members to assess the demonstration of their team values by completing the "Demonstrating Team Values" worksheet. Allow approximately ten minutes.

4. Ask team members to share their assessment of each value.

5. Develop agreement on which values are consistently demonstrated and which need more attention.

6. For each of the values that requires more attention, develop a team list of actions that need to be taken or behaviors demonstrated.

7. Ask team members to commit to taking the actions agreed to in order to strengthen the values.

8. Ask members to recap these commitments on the "Team Commitments to Action" worksheet provided (Handout 5.6.2), and to refer back to it regularly.

Outcome

A heightened awareness of key team values.

An understanding of which values require attention.

A commitment to taking actions required to strengthen the team's values.

Demonstrating Team Values

PARTICIPANT'S WORKSHEET

Value	Rate how well you believe the value is currently demonstrated (rate on a 1 to 10 scale where 1 = low and 10 = high)	List what you believe the team needs to do more of in order to strengthen the value	List what you believe the team should do less of to strengthen the value

From *Games Teams Play*, by Leslie Bendaly. © McGraw-Hill Ryerson 1996

Team Commitments to Action

PARTICIPANT'S WORKSHEET

Value: _____
In order to strengthen this value we will:

_____

_____

_____

_____

_____

_____

Value: _____
In order to strengthen this value we will:

_____

_____

_____

_____

_____

_____

Value: _____
In order to strengthen this value we will:

_____

_____

_____

_____

_____

_____

Value: _____
In order to strengthen this value we will:

_____

_____

_____

_____

_____

_____

HANDOUT 5.6.2

5.7 FOCUSING THE TEAM I: IDENTIFYING CRITICAL SUCCESS FACTORS ✪ ✪

Objectives
To help the team focus more clearly on priorities by clarifying the areas that require the greatest attention if the team is to achieve its goals.

Time Required: 1.5 hours +

Background
Teams frequently complain about being "too scattered" or "juggling too many balls" but don't know what to let go of and where to put their concentration. Without focus high performance eludes them.

High performance teams are clear about their critical success factors.

Critical success factors are areas that must receive attention. The strength of these factors determines the ultimate success of the team. If the team experiences success in the areas described by the critical success factors, it will inevitably reach its targets/goals.

Critical success factors reflect the nature and function of the team as well as its level of development. A sales team might list the following as some of its CSFs:

- Responsiveness to customers

- Product knowledge

- Maintaining relationships with suppliers

- Communication with head office

Materials Required
Provided: Overhead, Handout

Steps

1. Present the definition on Overhead 5.7.1.

2. Use the Technique for Developing and Organizing Ideas (page 9) to develop a list of the team's critical success factors. Limit the number to no more than seven, preferably five factors.

   Note: Remind participants that the critical success factors must be *critical*, i.e., the team cannot achieve its goals if the factor is weak.

3. Distribute the Critical Success Factors worksheet (Handout 5.7.1). Ask team members to complete the worksheet. (Allow 10 to 15 minutes.)

4. Invite members to share their observations.

5. Identify the CSFs that deserve more attention and develop commitments to action for strengthening them.

6. Check for consensus.

Outcome

A clear understanding of what is required for success.

A list of critical success factors.

Agreement on actions to be taken to strengthen critical success factors.

✔ **Cohesiveness**

CRITICAL SUCCESS FACTORS

Critical success factors are the limited number of areas to which a team must give full attention and achieve success if it is to reach its goals and fulfil its potential.

OVERHEAD 5.7.1

Critical Success Factors

PARTICIPANT'S WORKSHEET

Critical Success Factor	Attention presently given to this factor (rate on a 1 to 10 scale where 1 = low and 10 = high)	Recommendations for strengthening the critical success factor

5.8 FOCUSING THE TEAM II: MATCHING ACTIVITIES TO CRITICAL SUCCESS FACTORS ✪ ✪ ✪

Your Notes

Objectives

To determine if the team is focusing its time and energy appropriately.

To realign its focus if required.

Time Required: 1.5 hours

Background

This workout asks team members to match activities to priorities. To do so they must have a list of the team's critical success factors. If the team has not previously considered its CSFs, the workout "Focusing the Team I" should be completed first.

Materials Required

Provided: Handouts (2)
Other: A list of the team's critical success factors

Steps

1. Distribute the participant's worksheet, "Matching Activities to Critical Success Factors" (Handout 5.8.1). Ask each participant to make a list of:

   • The activities on which they spend most of their time.

   • Items on their to-do lists that always get relegated to the bottom and for which they never seem to have enough time. (Allow approximately ten minutes.)

2. Distribute a list of the team's critical success factors.

3. Ask participants to work in small groups (three to four participants) to match their activities to the team's list of critical success factors. Use the workout guidelines provided (Handout 5.8.2). (Allow approximately 30 minutes.)

4. Discuss their observations.

Discussion Questions

1) Do the activities on which team members spend most of their time contribute to strengthening the team's CSFs?

2) Are activities that sit at the bottom of team members' to-do lists important to the team's CSFs?

3) Are there any activities that haven't even made team members' to-do lists that are important to the team's CSFs?

4) Are there activities that the team should be dropping altogether?

5. Identify any commitments to action resulting from the discussion.

6. Check for consensus on the action items.

Outcome

A better understanding of how the team uses its time.

Agreements on how the team can best use its time.

Greater cohesiveness by ensuring all team members' activities can be related directly to the team's critical success factors.

Matching Activities to Critical Success Factors

PARTICIPANT'S WORKSHEET

List the activities that take most of your time:

_____

_____

_____

_____

_____

_____

List the activities that sit at the bottom of your "to-do list" and receive little of your time:

_____

_____

_____

_____

_____

_____

HANDOUT 5.8.1

From *Games Teams Play*, by Leslie Bendaly. © McGraw-Hill Ryerson 1996

Assessing Activities' Importance

WORKOUT GUIDELINES

Allotted time: 30 minutes

1. Examine each member's activities as they relate to the team's critical success factors.

   ◆ Which activities directly support the critical success factors?

   ◆ Are there any activities that do not directly support any critical success factor?

   ◆ Are there any activities at the bottom of the to-do lists that are important to any of the critical success factors?

   ◆ Are there any activities that are critical to the team's success that do not appear on any (or appear on only a few) to-do lists?

2. Be prepared to share with the larger group:

   (i) any activities that don't support critical success factors, and

   (ii) any activities that deserve more time.

From *Games Teams Play*, by Leslie Bendaly. © McGraw-Hill Ryerson 1996

5.9 ACTING TO... ✪ ✪

Your Notes

Objectives

To encourage creative thinking about how the team works and to identify opportunities for improvement.

Time Required: 30 minutes +

Background

Teams that thrive do not take their success for granted. They recognize that success is due not only to what they do but to how the team functions.

This activity challenges members to escape vertical thinking patterns and so explore aspects of the team's performance that normally would not be considered.

You are provided with a selection of quotations that will act as a catalyst for team members' thinking. The quotations are varied and will trigger different thoughts in different members.

Note: The following instructions present a version of the activity that uses all of the quotations provided. You may, however, opt to use fewer or even one quotation based on team needs and time available.

Materials Required

Provided: Overheads (3), Handout

Steps

1. Present the quotations to the group using Overhead 5.9.1.

2. Select one quotation and lead a mini-discussion.

Possible Question:
Does this quotation trigger any thoughts about your team?

This mini-discussion is meant to focus the group and to "prime the well" for the individual thinking that follows.

3. Provide each participant with a copy of the "According To..." worksheet (Handout 5.9.1). Allow approximately ten minutes for completion of the worksheet. Briefly review the instructions.

   Variation — Invite participants to complete this in small groups. Select or ask the group to select three or four quotations. Allow approximately 25 minutes.

4. Discuss each quotation, asking participants to share their responses.

5. Recap observations and any opportunities for improvement that evolve from this observation.

6. Lead the group in identifying which opportunities for improvement can be turned into commitments to action.

7. Check for consensus.

Outcome
Better understanding of one another's perspectives.

New perspectives on how the team works.

Commitments to action that will increase team effectiveness.

THOUGHTS FOR TEAMS

"In the knowledge society, managers (people) must prepare to abandon everything they know."

Peter Drucker

"Our Achilles Heel is not applying what we already know."

Leslie Bendaly

"What sets apart high performance teams is the degree of commitment, particularly how deeply committed the team members are to one another."

Jon R. Katzenbach
The Wisdom of Teams

✔ **Cohesiveness**

"Innovation is creative destruction."

Joseph Schumpeter
(Economist)

"Our age of anxiety is the result of trying to do today's job with yesterday's tools, with yesterday's concepts."

Marshall McCluhan

"You have to see the future to deal with the present."

Faith Popcorn

"It's not good enough to say we're doing our best, we must do what has to be done."

Winston Churchill

From *Games Teams Play*, by Leslie Bendaly. © McGraw-Hill Ryerson 1996

✔ **Cohesiveness**

"... there are powerful forces at work in organizations that tend to make the intelligence of the team less than, not greater than, the intelligence of individual team members. Many of these factors are within the direct control of the team members."

Peter Senge
The Fifth Discipline

OVERHEAD 5.9.3

According to…

PARTICIPANT'S WORKSHEET

Quotation	Thoughts About Your Team
"In the knowledge society, managers must prepare to abandon everything they know." *Peter Drucker*	
"Our Achilles Heel is not applying what we already know." *Leslie Bendaly*	
"What sets apart high performance teams is the degree of commitment, particularly how deeply committed the team members are to one another." *John R. Katzenbach* *The Wisdom of Teams*	
"Innovation is creative destruction." *Joseph Schumpeter* *(Economist)*	

HANDOUT 5.9.1

ACCORDING TO... (cont'd)

Quotation	Thoughts About Your Team
"Our age of anxiety is the result of trying to do today's job with yesterday's tools, with yesterday's concepts." *Marshall McCluhan*	
"You have to see the future to deal with the present." *Faith Popcorn*	
"It's not good enough to say we're doing our best, we must do what has to be done." *Winston Churchill*	
". . . there are powerful forces at work in organizations that tend to make the intelligence of the team less than, not greater than, the intelligence of individual team members. Many of these factors are within the direct control of the team members." *Peter Senge* *The Fifth Discipline*	

HANDOUT 5.9.1

5.10 TEAM SYNERGY I ✪

Your Notes

Objectives
To identify synergy as a team development goal.

To energize a team and have fun.

Time Required: 20 minutes +

Background
Once a team label has been applied to a group it is not unusual for the group to quickly forget why they are working as a team. The synergy created by effective teamwork is one of the important benefits of working as a team. Unless the team keeps this benefit in front of it and its members continually make an effort to develop in such a way as to reach this benefit, it is likely to elude them.

This workout consists of two activities that link. Each may stand alone. In Activity I participants are asked to use a game to construct a definition of team: "A team is greater than the sum of its parts." Activity I may stand alone if time is limited and/or your objective in using the activity is to highlight the concept of synergy while having fun as a team.

Activity II provides an opportunity for the team to explore the concept of synergy in greater depth and to examine their team in relation to it.

Materials Required
Provided: Overhead, Words of definition to be cut out

Steps

1. Display the "A TEAM IS" overhead (Overhead 5.10.1).

2. Explain to the group that you are going to ask them to complete this definition. Each person will be given a piece of paper with one word of the definition on it. You will ask everyone to stand and then look at the word on their paper. They must then move around and link with others who hold different words to complete the team definition. Their objective is to be the first group to construct and announce the definition.

3. Go through the above steps.

4. Briefly examine the definition and explain that this is also a definition of synergy and that synergy is what distinguishes high performance teams.

Discussion Question

Is your team achieving synergy?

Note: Ask for examples to back up responses.

If there is a need to increase synergy go to *Team Synergy II* that follows.

Outcome

A refocusing of the group on creating greater team synergy.

✔ **Cohesiveness**

A TEAM IS...

From *Games Teams Play*, by Leslie Bendaly. © McGraw-Hill Ryerson 1996

Cut out and fold:

greater

than

the

sum

of

its

parts

WORKOUT 5.10: Words of Definition

From *Games Teams Play*, by Leslie Bendaly. © McGraw-Hill Ryerson 1996

5.11 TEAM SYNERGY II ✪ ✪

Objectives
To increase team synergy.

Time Required: 1.5 hours +

Background
See Background to 5.10, *Team Synergy I*, page 231.

Materials Required
Provided: Handout

Steps

1. Distribute copies of the participant's worksheet, "Creating Synergy" (Handout 5.11.1).

2. Ask participants to work in groups of four to seven members to complete the workout.

3. Invite each group to share its output from the workout. (Allow 25 minutes.)

4. Recap common points.

Discussion Question

Considering these observations, what should the team do to increase its synergy?

Recap points made, check for consensus and commitment. Ask participants to record the commitments to action on the second page of their sheet where indicated.

Outcome
Commitments to action for increased team synergy.

Creating Synergy

PARTICIPANT'S WORKSHEET — GROUP

A team is greater than the sum of its parts.

Group Workout

Allotted time: 40 minutes

Instructions
1. Individually rate the following Team Synergy Indicators as to their strength within your team and identify opportunities for improvement (where 1 = low and 4 = high).

2. Share and discuss

3. Share ratings and discuss.

4. As a group identify opportunities for improvement.

Communication

We keep one another fully informed.   **1   2   3   4**

We use communication to create
synergy by looking for opportunities
to pass on "extra" information beyond
the basic need to know.   **1   2   3   4**

We communicate openly and
effectively with one another.   **1   2   3   4**

TOTAL SCORE _____

Opportunities for improvement

_____

_____

_____

HANDOUT 5.11.1

Creating Synergy (cont'd)   *Page 2 of 2*

Linking Roles

We understand one another's roles.   **1   2   3   4**

We recognize ways in which we can
link to increase team performance.   **1   2   3   4**

We use those links to enhance team
performance.   **1   2   3   4**

TOTAL SCORE _____

Opportunities for improvement

_____

_____

_____

Team Meetings

We meet frequently to examine team
performance and to look for ways of
working more effectively.   **1   2   3   4**

Meetings are productive. Members
leave feeling their time has been
well spent.   **1   2   3   4**

Ideas for improvement produced in
meetings are turned into action.   **1   2   3   4**

TOTAL SCORE _____

Opportunities for improvement

_____

_____

_____

Commitments to Action for Increasing Team Synergy
(to be completed with entire team)

_____

_____

_____

HANDOUT 5.11.1

_____

From *Games Teams Play*, by Leslie Bendaly. © McGraw-Hill Ryerson 1996

5.12 DEVELOPING INFLUENCING POWER ✪ ✪

Objectives

To increase team members' recognition of the importance of influence.

To identify groups and individuals within the organization whom the team needs to influence in order to be effective.

To heighten team members' awareness of the team's influencing ability.

To strengthen the team's ability to influence.

Time Required: 1.5 hours +

Background

The success of teams and individuals depends to a greater degree than ever on the ability to influence those around us. Authority is no longer the only determinate of who gets resources or who is listened to. Teams and individuals succeed by influencing others to support them in their endeavors.

In cross-functional teams, influencing skills must be particularly well honed. Members bring the perspectives of their function or work unit to the team and need to present them in such a way that they will ultimately have an impact on team outcomes. Members must also take decisions and information from their cross-functional team to their work unit and present this information in such a way that the work of the team will receive the support it needs.

High-performance teams must be aware of their influence targets (people and groups whom they must positively influence in order to achieve success) and regularly assess their effectiveness in influencing them.

Materials Required
Provided: Overheads (3).

Steps
1. Introduce this workout with a brief discussion of the need to influence if the team has not already identified the power to influence as a critical success factor.

2. Define Influence Targets (use Overhead 5.12.1).

3. Brainstorm to develop a list of the team's key influence targets.

4. For each target ask, "How do you think this target sees your team? If asked to describe your team what might he/she/they say?" Collect the responses on a flipchart under the heading "How Others See Us" or use the blank overhead titled "How Others See Us" (Overhead 5.12.2). Alternatively, ask team members to select the statements listed on Overhead 5.12.3 that they believe the target might use to describe the team.

5. Examine the "Others see us as" list and for each target look for opportunities for improvement (i.e., statements that were not selected or negative statements identified by participants).

   a) Look for common impressions that cross the lists and make appropriate commitments to action for increasing the team's influence throughout the organization.

b) Examine negative impressions of the team that are unique to a particular individual or group and identify changes that the team can make to correct those impressions.

6. Recap commitments to action and check for consensus.

Outcome

Heightened awareness of how a team's ability to influence affects its success.

Commitments to action that will increase the team's ability to influence.

✔ **Cohesiveness**
✔ **Team Members' Contribution**

INFLUENCE
TARGET

People and groups whom we must positively influence in order to achieve success.

From *Games Teams Play*, by Leslie Bendaly. © McGraw-Hill Ryerson 1996

✔ **Cohesiveness**
✔ **Team Members' Contribution**

HOW OTHERS SEE US

_____

_____

_____

_____

OTHERS SEE US AS:

- ◆ sensitive to their needs
- ◆ helpful
- ◆ anxious to provide superior service
- ◆ good listeners
- ◆ good communicators
- ◆ understanding of their points of view
- ◆ open to feedback
- ◆ flexible, honest
- ◆ assertive but not aggressive
- ◆ having expertise
- ◆ believable
- ◆ having a good track record
- ◆ committed to what we do
- ◆ wanting what's best for the organization
- ◆ delivering quality

OVERHEAD 5.12.3

5.13 GUIDING VALUES I: DEVELOPING GUIDING VALUES ✪ ✪

Objectives

To check the team's degree of cohesiveness.

To strengthen the team's cohesiveness.

To select a set of guiding values.

Time Required: 1 hour

Background

A team's cohesiveness depends on the degree of agreement on what the team is in place to do and how it should do it.

Underlying these agreements are the team members' work-related values. Therefore the greater the degree of consensus on these values, the greater the degree of cohesiveness.

Some teams consist of a group of members who are by nature "in sync" as to their values. It is very easy for these individuals to agree on a set of working values. Usually these groups see eye to eye and come to agreement on most decisions easily. This group has a high level of cohesiveness by nature. The downside may be that it may not always make quality decisions because of too much like thinking; this may go unnoticed because there is no team member who thinks differently.

Many teams are not highly cohesive by nature. That is, they do not have a group of team members who happen to think alike. These teams must work to develop cohesiveness but once they have, they will have the benefits of a high degree of cohesiveness within a group of people who do not all think alike. Different perspectives will therefore be brought to the table and the team will exhibit a greater tendency to challenge each other's thinking.

A high degree of cohesiveness is important for high performance teamwork, but it is most powerful when coupled with objectivity.

This activity provides teams the opportunity to check their natural degree of cohesiveness and build cohesiveness as required.

Note: This workout works best for small teams (three to eight members). Larger teams can be broken into smaller groups for the activity and agreements on values can be looked for between the subgroups, but the outcomes are not as powerful in this situation.

Materials Required
Provided: Overheads (2), Handout, Guiding Values cards.

Steps
Pre Workshop
Prepare a set of Guiding Values cards for each participant.

In the Workshop
1. Give each team member a set of Guiding Values cards.

2. Distribute the Developing Guiding Values workout guidelines (Handout 5.13.1).

3. Review the guidelines with the participants and explain the scoring and interpretation using Overhead 5.13.1.

4. Allow 25 minutes for the team to complete this activity. Explain that the teams will likely believe that each of the values is important. Their objective is to identify and agree to three values that require more consistent demonstration in their team (they are weak) and/or are particularly important at this time for some reason. For example, the team might say, "We need to emphasize participation more because of the enormous amount of change we are experiencing." or "We don't do a very good job of sharing the load."

5. Ask teams to share their sets of values, the rationale for their choice, their degree of cohesiveness, and how the activity benefited their team.

Outcome

Agreement on guiding values.

Better understanding of one another's work values.

A sharper team focus.

DEGREE OF COHESIVENESS INTERPRETATION

Circle your score

30　　25　　20　　15　　10　　5　　0

Highly cohesive by nature

Moderate cohesiveness

Low cohesiveness

Possible downside: Too much like thinking could jeopardize quality

Upside: Should bring different perspectives to the team. If well managed, these can enhance performance and outcomes

Teamwork expected to require vigilance

✔ **Cohesiveness**
✔ **Climate**

GUIDING VALUES

A set of values the demonstration of which is critical to the team's success.

Developing Guiding Values

WORKOUT GUIDELINES — GROUP

Allotted time: 25 minutes

Objective
To agree to the team's most important Guiding Values.

1. Ensure each team member has a full set of Values cards (seven different cards).

2. Individually select the three cards that indicate the values you believe need to be demonstrated more consistently in your team, or are particularly important at this time. Take time to reflect on this. Discard the remaining four cards face down.

3. At the group signal, lay down the three Values cards you have selected face up.

4. Individually describe your understanding of each value you selected. Give specific examples from your work environment that demonstrate the presence or absence of the value.

5. Give yourselves ten points for each value that was selected by all team members and for which there is consistent understanding (see score card).

6. Attempt to come to agreement on the values for which there was no initial agreement. Score five points for each value agreed to through dialogue (see score card).

7. Complete the "Cohesiveness Interpretation" (page 2 of 2).

From *Games Teams Play*, by Leslie Bendaly. © McGraw-Hill Ryerson 1996

DEGREE OF COHESIVENESS INTERPRETATION

Circle your score

30 **25** **20** **15** **10** **5** **0**

Highly cohesive   *Moderate*   *Low cohesiveness*
by nature   *cohesiveness*

Possible downside: Upside: Teamwork expected
Too much like   Should bring differ- to require vigilance
thinking could   ent perspectives to
jeopardize   the team. If well
quality   managed, these can
                       enhance perform-
                       ance and outcomes

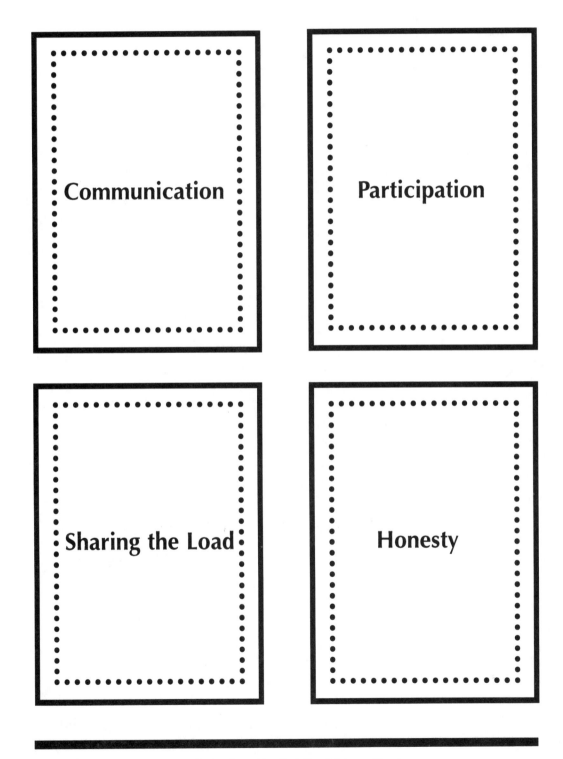

Communication

Participation

Sharing the Load

Honesty

WORKOUT 5.13: Guiding Values Cards

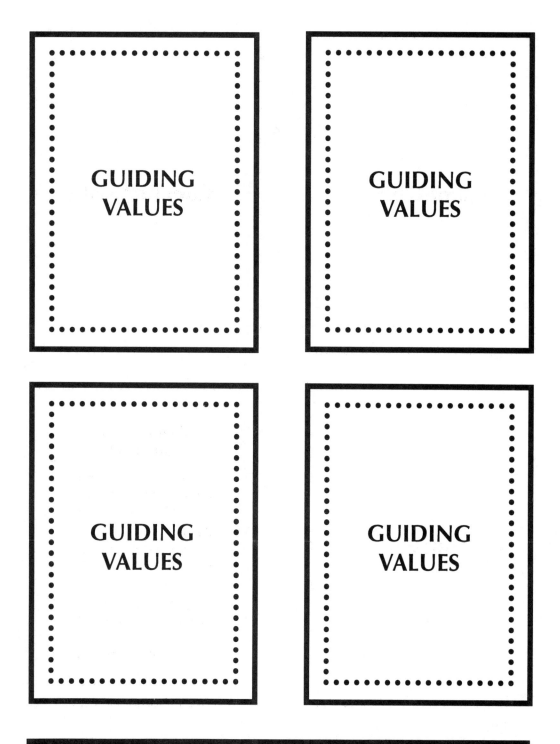

**GUIDING
VALUES**

**GUIDING
VALUES**

**GUIDING
VALUES**

**GUIDING
VALUES**

WORKOUT 5.13: Guiding Values Cards

Sensitivity

Commitment

Equality

Cohesiveness
Score Card

Value 1	Score
Immediate agreement	10
Negotiated agreement	5

Value 2	
Immediate agreement	10
Negotiated agreement	5

Value 3	
Immediate agreement	10
Negotiated agreement	5

Total Score _____

WORKOUT 5.13: Guiding Values Cards

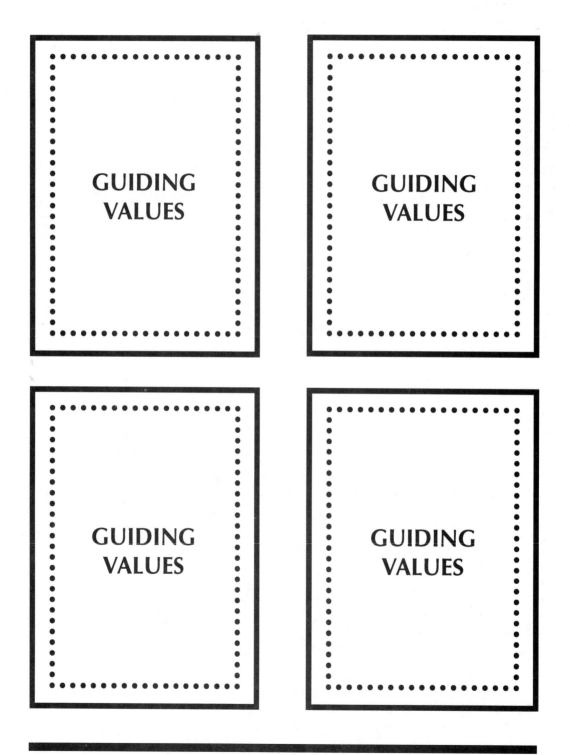

GUIDING VALUES

GUIDING VALUES

GUIDING VALUES

GUIDING VALUES

WORKOUT 5.13: Guiding Values Cards

5.14 GUIDING VALUES II: DEMONSTRATING GUIDING VALUES ✪ ✪

Your Notes

NOTE: *To be used with Guiding Values Workout I*

Objectives

To develop working agreements that will help to ensure that the team's set of guiding values is demonstrated.

To increase team cohesiveness.

Time Required: – 1 hour

Background

It is much easier to verbally agree to values than it is to consistently demonstrate them. This workout encourages the demonstration of common values.

Materials Required

Provided: Handout

Steps

1. Lead the team in developing team agreements for each of the team's three Guiding Values. For example:

   Guiding Value: honesty.

   Possible Team Agreement: If we have an issue with something someone has done, we will speak directly with the person responsible.

   You might use the Technique for Developing and Organizing Ideas (page 9) to do this.

   Note: If this is a multiple team workshop, distribute the "Demonstrating

Guiding Values" workout guidelines (Handout 5.14.1) (Alloted time: 20 minutes).

Discussion Question

What can you do to keep your agreements alive?

Common responses:
Review our agreements at meetings.

Take personal responsibility for living up to them.

Remind one another if we slip.

Recap and check for consensus.

Outcome
Working agreements that support the team's guiding values.

Increased team cohesiveness.

Demonstrating Guiding Values

WORKOUT GUIDELINES — GROUP

Developing Agreements

Allotted time: 20 minutes

Develop two team/working agreements for each of your team's guiding values, i.e., identify and agree to behaviors that would demonstrate/reflect each value.

e.g.　Guiding Value: honesty

Team Agreement: If we have an issue with something someone has done, we will speak directly to the person responsible.

Value: _____

Agreement: _____

_____

_____

Value: _____

Agreement: _____

_____

_____

Value: _____

Agreement: _____

_____

_____

5.15 GETTING IN TUNE ✪ ✪

Objectives

To increase the team's ability to pull together.

To ensure agreement on priorities and values.

Time Required: 1 hour +

Background

If a team is to pull together it must agree on what it should be doing and how it should be accomplishing its objectives.

Agreement on priorities and values is often assumed. Periodically checking whether all members are indeed in tune can bring about important realignment.

Materials Required

Provided: Handout

Steps

1. Distribute the "Developing Cohesiveness" worksheet (Handout 5.15.1) and review the instructions.

2. Allow approximately 10–15 minutes for its completion and ensure each member works independently.

3. Ask members to share their responses in each category.

4. Check for commonalities and differences and discuss the differences.

5. Lead the group to agreement on three values, three task priorities, and three critical success factors.

Note: The ease with which the team comes to consensus on these points is a reflection of the degree of cohesiveness within the team.

Outcome

A set of agreed-upon values, priorities, and critical success factors.

A better understanding of one another's perspectives concerning values and priorities.

Increased team cohesiveness.

Developing Cohesiveness

PARTICIPANT'S WORKSHEET

Respond to each of the following questions. Please work independently.

Values

Values reflect the way in which the team works and what it believes in. The team must demonstrate corporate values but may have additional values that are also important to its achieving success. List below the three values that you believe to be most critical to the team's success.

◆ _____

_____

_____

◆ _____

_____

_____

◆ _____

_____

_____

HANDOUT 5.15.1

Developing Cohesiveness (cont'd)

Priority Tasks

Consider the next three months in the life of the team. What do you believe to be the three most critical tasks for the team to be working on during this period?

◆ _____
  _____

◆ _____
  _____

◆ _____
  _____

Critical Success Factors

Critical success factors are the handful of areas in which the team must excel or put forth extra effort if it is to be successful. If these areas are well managed the tasks will be completed with ease. Critical success factors could include:

◆ Updating team members' skills

◆ Communicating effectively with head office

◆ Having a complete grasp of new legislation

◆ Responsiveness to customers

Critical success factors vary from team to team and may change as a team's needs and/or environment change.

List what you believe to be your team's three key success factors below:

1. _____

2. _____

3. _____

From *Games Teams Play*, by Leslie Bendaly. © McGraw-Hill Ryerson 1996

5.16 CHARADES FOR DEVELOPING TEAM FITNESS ✪

Objectives
To increase team members' recognition of the elements required to develop a fit team.

Time Required: 20 minutes +

Background
The Team Fitness Test measures the five elements — Shared Leadership, Group Work Skills, Climate, Cohesiveness, and Team Members' Contribution — that are critical to high performance teamwork. If the fitness elements are to be strong, team members must be working together to strengthen them. To do this members must first be aware of the elements and keep them in front of them.

This is most useful for groups that have at some time been introduced to the Team Fitness Test and have committed to ongoing team development.

Materials Required
Provided: Overhead, elements to be cut out
Other: Envelopes to hold the names of the five elements

Steps
Pre Workshop

1. Cut out names of the elements and put a set in each envelope (one envelope per group). If team is larger than eight members, plan to break into smaller groups of four to six.

In Workshop

1. Distribute the envelopes containing the elements.

2. Explain that the objective is for each team to identify/remember each of the five elements critical to high performance teamwork. They will receive help in doing this. Each team member will pull an element from the envelope and must communicate/act out the element to their team members without speaking.

   Quickly review some tips on how to play charades for those members to whom this may be new, e.g.,

   Words can be broken into syllables. Players can choose to act out a word that "sounds like" the element they are trying to communicate — agree on signs for these.

3. If working with more than one group, add an element of competition and time the groups.

4. Once each group has identified all five, briefly review them (using Overhead 5.16.1) and check for understanding of their meaning.

Outcome

Increased recognition of elements required for team fitness.

TEAM FITNESS ELEMENTS

Shared Leadership

Group Work Skills

Climate

Cohesiveness

Team Members' Contribution

Copy number of sets required, cut out and insert into envelopes:

Group Work Skills

Climate

Cohesiveness

Shared Leadership

Team Members' Contribution

WORKOUT 5.16: Team Fitness Elements

5.17 GETTING IN SYNC WITH THE NEW WORLD OF WORK ✪ ✪

Objectives

To clarify the types of behaviors and workstyles required for teams to thrive in the new world of work.

To check whether individual and team behaviors are consistent with the new requirements.

To make personal commitments to change that will enhance the team's ability to thrive in the new world of work.

Time Required: 1 hour

Background

Most teams demonstrate an intellectual understanding of what is required in order to excel in the new world of work. Not all teams, however, consistently demonstrate appropriate behavior.

The industrial-based economy was driven by the production of goods and most employment was related directly to production. The new economy is driven by technology, information, and innovation. The employment focus is on knowledge workers and service providers. Two very different organizational models and sets of practices are needed to support the two different economies.

The traditional organization that worked well enough in the old economy cannot respond to today's needs. Teams are the foundation and the heart of the new flexible organization. This workout challenges teams as to whether their behaviors reflect those required for "thrival" in the new world. Too often organizations have re-organized and stuck the label of team on every work unit and task force. Few, however, are behaving very differently from the way they did before. The net result—huge investment with no return.

Although companies are renovating, in some cases gutting their traditional organization, remnants of it still exist in most companies and may continue to do so for some time. In some companies, old and new practices exist side by side, although often not comfortably. Gradually the new will "take" and eventually replace the traditional.

The following characteristics describe the traditional organization.

Vertical. Most power is held in the hands of management. Power comes from authority, the power to make decisions, and from access to information. Communication is limited and primarily top down. The traditional organization is designed and works vertically (decision making, communication, departments, and functions).

Inward looking. The traditional organization tends to be inward looking. For example it focuses more on "what *we* did last year" or "what *we* know to be best" rather than being in tune with the environment, customers, competitors, etc.

Focused on task. Expectations of employees in the traditional organization were: Keep your head down; keep your eye on the task; think about what you are doing, not how you are doing it.

Expectations of employees were often limited to meeting minimum performance as indicated in the job description. They were expected to bring their bodies to work and just enough of their minds to get the job done. For the most part, organizational practices sent the message, "We've hired your body, leave your mind (ideas) at home."

The flexible organization balances the focus on the task (what) and the process (how). Teams are clear about and committed to the team task but know when to stop to examine the team process, including the way decisions are made, how well meetings work, and the dynamics of the team.

Note: The Team Fitness Test supports teams in examining the team process.

People and work are isolated in compartments. In the traditional organization, jobs, people, and functions are compartmentalized and vertical barriers are the norm. The result is what we often refer to as "silos".

In the flexible organization there is awareness of working in a system, that everything an individual and his or her team does, directly or indirectly, immediately or in the longer term affects the rest of the organization.

In order to thrive in the new economy, companies and their people must develop models and practices that demonstrate the opposite of almost everything that was the norm in the traditional organization.

Materials Required
Provided: Overhead, Handouts (2)

Steps

1. Examine the differences between the old world and the new using Overhead 5.17.1.

2. Distribute the "Transition from the Old World of Work to the New" worksheet (Handout 5.17.1).

3. Ask team members to complete the worksheet individually. Allow approximately ten minutes.

4. Ask participants to share their observations.

Note: The facilitator may have to challenge participants' thinking. It is easy for participants to say "Yes, we are doing everything we need to do" and to find only a small example to support their claim.

Discussion Question

What can team members do to ensure that the team is functioning in a way that is consistent with the requirements of the new world of work?

From the responses develop a list of commitments to action. Recap and check for consensus.

Optional
Distribute the "Personal Commitments for Thriving in the New World of Work" worksheet (Handout 5.17.2). Let participants know that you will be asking each of them to share one personal commitment with the team.

Outcome

A better understanding of the team's synchronicity in the new world of work.

Commitments to action that will support the team's functioning with increased effectiveness.

Personal commitments to changing behaviors to better match the requirements of the information age. (If participants have completed the "Personal Commitments for Thriving in the New World of Work" worksheet.)

The Industrial-Based Economy	*The Information-Based Economy*
Characteristics of The Rigid Organization	**Characteristics of The Flexible Organization**
Vertical	Horizontal
Inward looking	Outward looking
Focused on task	Balances focus on task and process
People and work isolated in compartments	People and work are part of a system or network

The Transition from the Old World of Work to the New

PARTICIPANT'S WORKSHEET

Examine the characteristics of the old world of work and the new. For each characteristic that you believe to be demonstrated in your team give examples of behaviors/actions/decisions made that you believe reflect that characteristic.

Traditional behaviors and characteristics (what worked in the Industrial-Based Economy)

Inward looking
Evidence: _____

_____

Vertical
Evidence: _____

_____

Focused on task
Evidence: _____

_____

People and work isolated in compartments
Evidence: _____

_____

HANDOUT 5.17.1

Behaviors and Characteristics of Information Age Organizations

Outward looking
Evidence: _____

_____

Horizontal
Evidence: _____

_____

Balances focus on task (what) and process (how)
Evidence: _____

_____

People and work are part of a system or network
Evidence: _____

_____

Indicate the degree to which you believe your team to be functioning in sync with the new world of work.

Old world of work   **New world of work**

1   2   3   4   5   6   7   8   9   10

Personal Commitments for Thriving in the New World of Work

PARTICIPANT'S WORKSHEET

Consider the characteristics of the old world of work and the new. Are there any ways in which you are "stuck" in the old world? Are there any behaviors you need to change to be in better sync with the new world and so make it easier to thrive in the new world?

Please list below personal commitments to action for thriving in the new world of work.

_____

_____

_____

_____

_____

_____

_____

_____

_____

_____

Team Fitness Element:
SHARED LEADERSHIP

SHARED LEADERSHIP

Shared leadership requires that:

- Team members are well informed.

- Each member fully participates.

- Each member has an equal voice. (In particular decisions some members may have more influence than others because of particular experience, skills, etc., however, all input is valued.)

- Team members share decision making as appropriate.

WORKOUTS

	Title	Level of Difficulty	Time Required	Page Number
6.1	The Color of Influence	✪ ✪	30 mins.+	295
6.2	Towards Increased Self-Direction	✪ ✪	45 mins.	299
6.3	Mountain Adventure	✪	45 mins.	307
6.4	Strengthening Shared Leadership in Traditional Teams	✪ ✪	1 hour+	313
6.5	Strengthening Shared Leadership in Self-Directed Teams	✪ ✪	1 hour+	323

6.1 THE COLOR OF INFLUENCE ✪ ✪

Objectives

To determine the degree to which team members feel they have influence/power within the team.

To clarify perceptions of influence.

Time Required: 30 minutes +

Background

A sense of shared leadership and influence are key to high performance teams. If members feel they have no influence or considerably less influence than others in team decisions, it is unlikely they will feel a sense of ownership for the success of the team.

This workout asks members to consider the degree to which they feel they have influence within the team. If influence is seen as unbalanced, the team explores why, and determines how a greater equalization of voices can be achieved.

Note: If the team going through the workout is a traditional one, i.e., it has a leader (supervisor or manager) appointed by the organization, the leader should be prepared for this activity. If team members do not feel they have power, it may be due to the leader's style and the leader must be open to exploring this possibility.

Materials Required

Red, green, blue and yellow paper squares or circles, about 2" x 2" (50 cm x 50 cm) (one of each color for each participant)

Two envelopes for each participant, one containing the colored squares, and one labelled "Response" (ensure colors cannot be easily seen through the envelope)

Steps

1. Distribute the envelopes.

2. Explain to the participants that in one envelope they will find four colored squares — one red, one green, one blue and one yellow. Ask them to consider the degree to which they feel they have influence within the team and to select a colored square according to the following:

   Red   — I have a great deal of influence

   Green — I have quite a bit of influence
   Blue   — I have little influence
   Yellow — I have no influence

   Put the above on a flipchart, board, etc.

   Give participants sufficient time to seriously consider their response.

   Note: Ensure participants are seated far enough apart to be able to select a color privately. Ask participants to put the colored square they select into the envelope labelled "Response".

3. Collect the Response envelopes.

4. Ask the participants what they considered when determining their degree of influence. Record responses on a board or flipchart.

   Common responses:

   Whether my opinion is asked.
   Whether my ideas are listened to.

Whether outcomes are influenced by my input.

5. Stick the squares to a board or flipchart sheet, putting like colors close together.

6. Describe the pattern suggested, e.g., "Most people feel they have a good deal of influence but a few feel they have little influence".

Discussion Questions

1) Why might this be the case?

2) How does this affect team outcomes?

3) Does this pattern and/or discussion suggest anything that the team or team members should be doing differently.

7. Identify potential commitments to action that have come out of the discussion and check for agreement.

Outcome

A tabling of possible issues related to power and influence.

Commitments that will help to ensure that all voices are heard.

6.2 TOWARDS INCREASED SELF-DIRECTION ✪ ✪

Objectives

To increase the team's level of self-direction.

To establish increased participation and self-direction as a team development goal.

Time Required: 45 minutes

Background

As teams move from traditional modes towards increased self-direction it is important that the team's level of authority be clearly understood. This may differ from task to task and will change as the team develops. The level of authority can be defined by the Levels of Influence following.

Levels of Influence

3   Team decides without Leader

2   Consensus—Team and Leader share the decision

Increased Self-Direction

1   Leader decides with input from Team

0   Leader decides

A team leader could define his or her primary responsibility as the continuous development of the team towards increased self-direction.

Note: This activity is effective only if the team leader is ready, willing, and able to "let go" and empower team members.

Materials Required
Provided: Overhead, Handout

Steps

1. Introduce team members to the Levels of Influence using Overhead 6.2.1.

2. Distribute the Levels of Influence workout guidelines (Handout 6.2.1). Allow ten minutes for its completion.

3. Ask team members to share their observations and from this output develop a list of decisions made at a level 0 or 1 that could have benefited by being made at a 2 or 3.

Discussion Questions

1) What benefits would be reaped by moving these types of decisions to a higher level?

2) What do you need to do to ensure that the team increases the frequency with which it works at the higher levels?

Common responses:

We must continue to develop skills to enable us to function effectively at higher levels of influence.

When we see an opportunity to be functioning at a higher level we must bring it to the leader's and the team's attention.

We must be willing to take the responsibility and accountability that go with increased authority.

Recap the discussion and check for consensus on any commitments to action made.

Outcome

Increased understanding of the team's opportunities for increased self-direction.

The recognition of increased self-direction as a goal of the team development process.

Commitments to action to support the team's development towards increased self-direction.

Your Notes

LEVELS OF INFLUENCE

3 Team decides without Leader

2 Consensus—Team and Leader

**1 Leader decides with
input from Team**

0 Leader decides

From *Games Teams Play*, by Leslie Bendaly. © McGraw-Hill Ryerson 1996

Levels of Influence

WORKOUT GUIDELINES

Allotted time: 10 minutes

Identify a decision that your team recently made at a 0 or 1 level that would have benefited from a level 2 or 3 process. Jot down the benefits that would have been experienced.

Decision:

_____

_____

_____

Level made at:

_____

_____

_____

Recommended level:

_____

_____

_____

Benefits:

_____

_____

_____

HANDOUT 6.2.1

6.3 MOUNTAIN ADVENTURE* ✪

Elements Strengthened:
Shared Leadership,
Team Members' Contribution,
and Group Work Skills

Your Notes

Objectives
To illustrate the importance of full participation in team decision making.

To heighten the awareness of the quality of participation in the team.

Time Required: 45 minutes

Background
Full participation is required for a sense of shared leadership. When the participation process is effective all input is valued and influences outcomes as appropriate. Team members feel a sense of ownership.

Materials Required
Provided: Handouts (2)

Steps

1. Distribute the workout guidelines (Handout 6.3.1).

2. Appoint an observer to each group, distribute the observer's worksheet (Handout 6.3.2), and discuss the instructions with the observers.

3. Allow groups 20 minutes to complete the task.

4. Compare groups' lists to the experts' list (provided on Handout 6.3.2).

---

* The author wishes to thank Dean and Judy Robinson for providing the information and insight that created this activity.

5. Allow approximately 15 minutes for the sharing and discussion of observer's comments. Ask the teams to identify how they can improve their participation process and to make appropriate commitments to action.

6. If more than one team is participating, ask teams to share their commitments to action with the larger group.

Note: If the team would benefit from examining the decision-making process add a discussion on the importance of developing criteria (for working to solution). Identifying criteria not only contributes to quality decisions but also facilitates consensus.

Outcome

Increased awareness as to the importance of the participation process.

Commitments to action to enhance the team's participation process.

Improve decision-making skills (if decision-making criteria are emphasized as in Notes above).

Mountain Adventure

WORKOUT GUIDELINES

You are members of a mountaineering expedition to the top of Mount McKinley in Alaska (1,948 feet (6,194 metres)). You are about halfway to the peak. A snowslide has injured two team members and a storm is moving in.

The group has decided to stay where it is.

One of you has volunteered to start down for help. You believe he/she can make some progress before the storm hits. He/she will have to bivouac (spend the night on the mount) alone. The volunteer must travel quickly and therefore lightly.

He/she can carry 14 items. As a group, select the items he/she should take with him/her from the 37 items he/she is now carrying.

Assume that he/she will also be carrying all of the essential climbing gear, including ropes, slings, ice axe and hammer, climbing harness, rock pitons, etc.

He/she is wearing:

Plastic climbing boots with padded inners

Gaiters (to keep snow out of boots)

Fleece jacket

Fleece trousers

Fleece Balaclava hat

Waterproof mittens with fleece liners

Thermal underwear

Socks

HANDOUT 6.3.1

From *Games Teams Play,* by Leslie Bendaly. © McGraw-Hill Ryerson 1996

Select 14 items from the following list:

Shovel	Tarp
Waterproof trousers	Large polythene bag (big enough for a person to get into)
Ski poles	
Compass	Sunglasses
Light propane stove	Bivouac brush (for brushing snow off clothes and sleeping bags)
Cooking pot	
Swiss Army knife	Hand flares
Large tin mug	Instant food packs
Spoon	Sunscreen
Toilet paper	Spare mitts
Map	Gloves
Down sleeping bag with waterproof exterior	Camera
	Film
Altimeter	Matches
Pad for sleeping bag	Whistle
Tent	Wineskin with wine
Windproof jacket with hood	Chocolate bars
First aid kit	Water bottle
Pied d'elephant (half a sleeping bag to cover lower limbs)	Hot chocolate in packages
	Pencil and paper in polythene bag
Headlamp with lithium batteries	Instant food pack

From *Games Teams Play*, by Leslie Bendaly. © McGraw-Hill Ryerson 1996

Mountain Adventure

OBSERVER'S ROLE

Consider the following:

1. Did everyone actively participate?

2. Was everyone heard?

3. Were any ideas lost?

4. Did some individuals have greater influence?

5. What gave these individuals greater influence?
   e.g.   Their position in the team? Mountaineering experience?
   A persuasive manner? Confidence? Aggression?

6. What decision-making methods were used?

7. Did the team reach consensus? i.e. Everyone fully supported
   the outcome. If yes, what helped them reach consensus?

If no, what hindered them?

From *Games Teams Play*, by Leslie Bendaly. © McGraw-Hill Ryerson 1996

Mountain Adventure

OBSERVER'S WORKSHEET

The Solution

Decision-Making Criteria

The following priorities must be considered in selecting items in this type of a mountaineering situation:

Keeping dry

Keeping warm (maintaining internal body temperature)

Knowing where you are

Ensuring you are prepared for possible damaging sun or snow glare

Note: Wine should not be on your list because alcohol worsens hypothermia.

Experts' recommended top 14 items:

Compass
Map
Instant food packs
Headlamp with lithium batteries
Sunglasses
Sunscreen
Down sleeping bag with waterproof exterior
Water bottle
Propane stove
Large tin mug
Swiss Army knife
Matches
Waterproof trousers
Windproof jacket with hood

6.4 STRENGTHENING SHARED LEADERSHIP IN TRADITIONAL TEAMS ✪ ✪

Note: Traditional team refers to a team whose leader is appointed by the organization and may be titled team leader, supervisor or manager.

Objectives

To check the degree of shared leadership within the team.

To identify opportunities for increasing the degree of shared leadership.

To make commitments to increasing the degree of shared leadership.

Time Required: 1 hour +

Background

Shared leadership is the key to a sense of ownership for the success of the team. In traditional teams, in which the leader is appointed (perhaps titled manager or supervisor), the degree of shared leadership is dependent on:

- The leader's recognition of the advantages of "letting go", including sharing decisions and passing on responsibilities traditionally held by the supervisor/manager.

- Ongoing development of team members to ensure they are capable of sharing leadership.

Your Notes

- Team members' recognition of contributing to the success of the whole team, including contributing ideas, voicing concerns, sharing decisions, and taking responsibility for outcomes, as part of the job.

Strengthening shared leadership challenges the team to examine all of these factors.

Materials Required

Provided: Handout, a set of "Shared Leadership" statements and numbered markers for each group

Other: An envelope for each group

Steps

1. Cut out "Shared Leadership" statements and numbered markers and place in envelope (use card or Bristol board for markers).

2. Distribute an envelope containing shared leadership statements, markers 1, 2, 3 and 4 and workout guidelines (Handout 6.4.1) to each group.

3. If team is larger than eight members, break into smaller groups of four to six members.

4. Allow approximately 25 minutes for the groups to complete the task.

5. If you have broken the team into more than one group, share the outcomes from each group and look for consensus on four to seven commitments to action.

Outcome

Commitments to action for increasing the degree of shared leadership within the team.

Strengthening Shared Leadership

WORKOUT GUIDELINES — GROUP

1. As a team, examine the shared leadership statements.

2. Rate each statement as it applies to your team by putting it in one of four possible piles (markers numbered 1 to 4 provided):

   1 – This does not apply to our team at all
   2 – This applies to our team to some degree
   3 – This applies to our team for the most part
   4 – Yes, this definitely describes our team

3. Identify the three statements which require the greatest improvement (from pile 1, 2, or 3).

4. Identify and agree to a specific action that can be taken by the team to move each statement chosen to a "4" and list below.

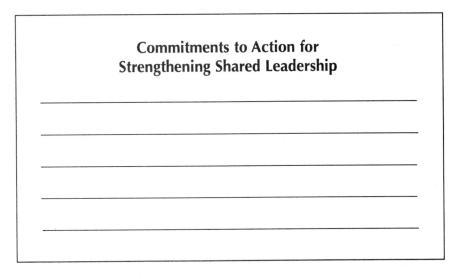

**Commitments to Action for
Strengthening Shared Leadership**

_____

_____

_____

_____

_____

From *Games Teams Play*, by Leslie Bendaly. © McGraw-Hill Ryerson 1996

The leader shares decision
making whenever possible
and appropriate.

The leader looks for
opportunities to pass on tasks
and responsibilities
usually held by the leader to
other team members.

Team members
participate fully.

WORKOUT 6.4: Shared Leadership Statements in Traditional Teams

From *Games Teams Play*, by Leslie Bendaly. © McGraw-Hill Ryerson 1996

Team members readily take on new responsibilities.

All team members have influence.

Team members are receiving the skills development opportunities required to be able to effectively share the leadership (i.e., share decisions and take on what have traditionally been management tasks).

WORKOUT 6.4: Shared Leadership Statements in Traditional Teams

Each team member sees the
success of the whole team
(not merely the success of their
immediate area of responsibility)
as a shared responsibility.

Markers

1

2

3

4

From *Games Teams Play,* by Leslie Bendaly. © McGraw-Hill Ryerson 1996

6.5 STRENGTHENING SHARED LEADERSHIP IN SELF-DIRECTED TEAMS ✪ ✪

Objectives

To check the degree of shared leadership within the team.

To identify opportunities for increasing the degree of shared leadership.

To develop commitments to increasing the degree of shared leadership.

Time Required: 1 hour +

Background

Shared leadership is the key to a sense of ownership for the success of the team. In a self-directed team, shared leadership requires:

- equal influence

- clear parameters of the team's accountability and authority

- full participation

- a sense of equal responsibility for the success of the team

Materials Required

Provided: Handout, a set of "Shared Leadership" statements and numbered markers for each group
Other: An envelope for each group

Steps

1. Cut out "Shared Leadership" statements and markers and place in envelopes (use card or Bristol board for markers).

2. Distribute an envelope of shared leadership statements, numbered markers and workout guidelines (Handout 6.5.1) to each group.

3. If team is larger than eight members, break into smaller groups of four to six members.

4. Allow approximately 25 minutes for the workout.

5. If you have broken the team into more than one group, share the outcomes from each group and look for consensus on four to seven commitments to action.

Outcome
Commitments to action for increasing the degree of shared leadership within the team.

Strengthening Shared Leadership

WORKOUT GUIDELINES — GROUP

1. As a team, examine the shared leadership statements.

2. Rate each statement as it applies to your team by putting it in one of four possible piles (markers numbered 1 to 4 provided):

   1 – This does not apply to our team at all
   2 – This applies to our team to some degree
   3 – This applies to our team for the most part
   4 – Yes, this definitely describes our team

3. Identify the three statements which require the greatest improvement (from pile 1, 2, or 3).

4. Identify and agree to a specific action that can be taken by the team to move each statement chosen to a "4" and list below.

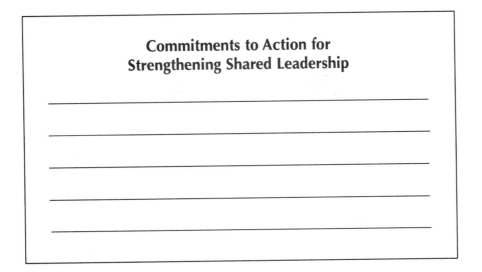

**Commitments to Action for
Strengthening Shared Leadership**

We each have equal
influence.

The team's parameters of
authority are clear.

The team's mandate and
accountability are clear.

WORKOUT 6.5: Shared Leadership Statements in Self-Directed Teams

Each member takes responsibility for the success of the team (not only his or her own area of responsibility).

We keep one another fully informed.

Each member participates fully in team decision making.

From *Games Teams Play*, by Leslie Bendaly. © McGraw-Hill Ryerson 1996

Each team member makes
team meetings a priority.

Markers

1

2

3

4

From *Games Teams Play,* by Leslie Bendaly. © McGraw-Hill Ryerson 1996

CHAPTER
7

Team Fitness Element:
TEAM MEMBERS' CONTRIBUTION

TEAM MEMBERS' CONTRIBUTION

Team members' contribution refers to team members' understanding of what is expected of them as team members and the degree to which they fulfil that expectation. Expectations of team members includes that they share information, communicate openly with one another, share the load, actively participate, demonstrate commitment to the team's goals and values, take equal responsibility for the success of the team, and recognize the degree to which individual behaviors affect the effectiveness of the team.

WORKOUTS

7.1 TWO HEADS ARE BETTER ✪

Objective
To heighten team members' awareness of the benefits of teamwork.

Time Required: 20 minutes

Background
The benefits of teamwork are more clearly understood when members can compare the experience of completing an activity independently and performing it as a team.

This workout can be used as an introduction to a team development session or as a stand alone activity for a new team whose members have not had a great deal of formal team experience.

Materials Required
Provided: Overheads (2)

Steps
1. Display the brainteasers from Overhead 7.1.1.

2. Give team members a few minutes to solve the riddles individually. When most participants have solved five or six of them, move to step 3.

3. Ask participants to move into groups of four to six members to complete the task.

4. Allow the groups to work until at least one group has solved all of the brainteasers.

5. Ask the groups to share their solutions. If useful display the answers using Overhead 7.1.2.

6. **Discussion Questions**

i) How did your experience in working on this activity independently compare with working in a group?

Common response:
When working in a group, we had more fun; it was easier to come up with the solutions; there was more energy.

ii) What were the additional benefits?

Common responses:
People brought different perspectives, experience, and skills to the task.

We were able to come up with more and more creative solutions.

We were more motivated to succeed.

iii) Were there any downsides to working in a group?

Common response:
No

Occasional responses:
Working in a group was too noisy and confusing.

I do better thinking on my own.

7. In summation, emphasize that teams offer many advantages but that in order to reap the benefits a team must work effectively and this requires the development of teamwork skills.

Outcome
A list of the benefits of teamwork and an understanding that teams that reap these benefits don't just happen; they are developed.

BRAINTEASERS

1. $\dfrac{\text{Step}}{\text{it}}$

2. **Sign**

3. S
   T
   O |
   ___RE

4. $\dfrac{\text{o}}{\begin{array}{c}\text{PhD}\\\text{MD}\\\text{MBA}\end{array}}$

5. cake (upside down)

6. I 4 I

7. $\dfrac{\text{dec}}{\text{ision}}$

8. **PROM   ISE**

9. (cube in circle with arrow)

10. ↑ L L I H

11. R   A
    O   D

12. C
    H
    CHECK
    C
    K

13. CHUTE   CHUTE

14. 4' —
    3' —
    2' —
    1' — STOP

✔ **Team Members' Contribution**
✔ **Cohesiveness**

BRAINTEASERS
Answers

1. **Step on it**
2. **Sign Post**
3. **Corner store**
4. **3 degrees below zero**
5. **Upside down cake**
6. **An eye for an eye**
7. **Split decision**
8. **Broken promise**
9. **Around the block**
10. **Up hill**
11. **Bumpy road**
12. **Cross check**
13. **Parachute**
14. **Short stop**

From *Games Teams Play*, by Leslie Bendaly. © McGraw-Hill Ryerson 1996

7.2 STRENGTHENING PERSONAL INFLUENCING ABILITIES ✪ ✪

Your Notes

Objectives

To increase team members' awareness of the impact of their personal influencing skills on the success of the team.

To challenge team members to identify opportunities for strengthening their influencing skills and to develop commitments to doing so.

Time Required: 30 minutes +

Background

See background for workout 5.12 "Developing Influencing Power" (page 243). The ability of the team to influence its targets is dependent on the influencing abilities of each team member. Influencing abilities are determined by the individual's personal organizational credibility (how they are viewed by others) and their personal influencing skills.

This workout challenges team members to assess their ability to influence others and to identify opportunities for growth.

Materials Required

Provided: Handout

Steps

1. The information under "Background", above, may be used as an introduction to this workout.

2. Distribute the Influencing Abilities Assessment (Handout 7.2.1) and allow 10 to 15 minutes for its completion.

Tip: If the team is sufficiently mature to allow members to give one another honest feedback, go to step 3. If not, go to step 4. You might want to repeat the activity in its entirety at a later time when the team is more mature and members would benefit from feedback from one another.

3. Distribute a second copy of "Influencing Abilities Assessment", ask members to work in pairs and again complete the assessment, this time with their partner in mind. Ask participants to compare their self-assessment with how their partners see them and look for strengths and opportunities for growth.

4. Ask participants to identify and share at least one influencing strength and one opportunity for growth to which they will commit to working on.

Outcome

A heightened understanding of the effect of personal influencing ability on team success.

A heightened understanding of personal influencing abilities.

Personal commitment to the development of influencing ability.

Influencing Abilities Assessment

PARTICIPANT'S WORKSHEET

Rate yourself on a 1 to 4 scale for each of the following statements, where

1 = I am not viewed positively in this area, and
4 = I am viewed exceptionally highly in this area.

A. Personal Organizational Credibility

1. **Competence**
   – The ability to do the job.　　　　**1　2　3　4**

2. **Discretion**
   – The ability to discern when it is or is not
   appropriate to comment or pass on
   information.　　　　**1　2　3　4**

3. **Attitude**
   – Ability to maintain a positive attitude
   even in negative circumstances.　　　**1　2　3　4**

4. **Honesty and Openness**
   – People feel they always know where I
   stand and can therefore trust me.　　**1　2　3　4**

5. **Track Record**
   – I have convinced people to move in
   certain directions/accept ideas in the past
   which proved to be very successful.　**1　2　3　4**

B. Personal Influencing Skills

1. Communication
a) I present my case/ideas clearly.   **1   2   3   4**

b) I present my case/ideas in such a way as
to increase the receptivity of the listener
(I don't turn them off or put them to
sleep).   **1   2   3   4**

2. Assertiveness
– I "hold my own" when appropriate,
without being aggressive.   **1   2   3   4**

3. Listening
– I listen effectively and respond to or use
what I hear when possible, e.g., build on
the ideas, address needs expressed.   **1   2   3   4**

4. Sensitivity
– I am sensitive to others' positions and
needs and demonstrate this in the way I
deal with people.   **1   2   3   4**

5. Enthusiasm
– I get enthused/excited/have a strong
feeling of commitment about new ideas
that I believe in and communicate this
enthusiasm to others.   **1   2   3   4**

From *Games Teams Play*, by Leslie Bendaly. © McGraw-Hill Ryerson 1996

7.3 CHANGE COMPATIBILITY ✪

Objective

To heighten participants' awareness of how quickly people become comfortable with the status quo, how even small change can make us uncomfortable, and of personal change compatibility.

Time Required: 5 minutes

Background

The setting for this activity is a team workshop or meeting. Use within 15 minutes after people have taken their seats.

Materials Required

None

Steps

1. Ask participants to please gather their materials and move to another seat.

2. Ask the following questions:

   • Who welcomed the idea when I suggested moving seats?

   • Who were indifferent?

   • Who felt at least slight discomfort or objection?

3. Discussion Question:
   What does this brief activity illustrate?

Common responses:

We each respond differently to change.

We quickly "settle in".

Many of us really prefer the status quo.

Sometimes we accept large changes more readily than small ones.

We all respond differently to change.

7.4 LEARNING THE PERSONAL BALANCING ACT ✪ ✪

Objectives

To increase awareness of the importance of balancing task-oriented and process-oriented behaviors if individuals and teams are to thrive in today's work environment.

To increase individual team members' awareness of their personal task/process balance.

To challenge team members to adjust personal behavior to better achieve a task/process balance.

Time Required: 35 minutes

Background

See background from 3.6 "Learning the Balancing Act" (page 85).

Materials Required

Provided: Handouts (2)

Steps

1. Introduce the concept of the task/process balance and its importance in teamwork.

2. Distribute the workout guidelines and worksheet (Handouts 7.4.1 and 7.4.2). Briefly review the workout guidelines. Emphasize there is no right or wrong workstyle. Allow ten minutes for the completion of the assessment.

3. Ask participants to form pairs and to continue the workout according to the guidelines. Allow 15 minutes.

4. Ask participants to share any recognitions they have made about their workstyle.

Your Notes

Learning the Personal Balancing Act

WORKOUT GUIDELINES

Allotted time: 25 minutes

1. Individually complete the Personal Workstyle Assessment.

2. Select a partner, someone who knows your workstyle and whose workstyle you know.

3. Share the characteristics you have each selected on the Workstyle Assessment.

4. Give one another feedback based on the following:

   ◆ Do you agree with the descriptors selected by your partner?

   ◆ Which of your partner's characteristics do you believe best support the team?

   ◆ Are any of your partner's characteristics so strongly demonstrated that they at any time hinder the team?

HANDOUT 7.4.1

From *Games Teams Play*, by Leslie Bendaly. © McGraw-Hill Ryerson 1996

Personal Workstyle Assessment

PARTICIPANT'S WORKSHEET

You will notice that characteristics described under the headings "Task Oriented" and "Process Oriented" are opposite. Put a check mark beside the statements that best describe the way you most often *prefer* to work i.e., how you are most comfortable working.

Task-Oriented Characteristics	Process-Oriented Characteristics
I . . .	I . . .
❏ Enjoy routine	❏ Work best in non-routine environment
❏ Can easily categorize things as black and white	❏ Believe many things fall in a grey area
❏ Enjoy focusing on details	❏ Like to focus on the big picture
❏ Like structure	❏ Dislike structure
❏ Use a "one thing at a time" approach to work	❏ Prefer to do several things simultaneously
❏ Prefer to base decisions on facts and figures	❏ Often make decisions based on intuition
❏ Have strongly formed opinions	❏ Readily see others' points of view
❏ Make quick decisions based on my own perception/opinion	❏ Thoroughly explore various perspectives before making decisions
❏ Prefer to use logic in problem solving	❏ Prefer creative problem-solving methods
❏ Prefer working alone	❏ Prefer working with others

HANDOUT 7.4.2

Personal Workstyle Assessment (cont'd)

PARTICIPANT'S WORKSHEET

1. Based on the above, would you describe yourself as more task oriented, process oriented or balanced?*

2. Which characteristics do you believe help you to best contribute to teamwork?

3. Do you demonstrate any characteristics so strongly that they might hinder teamwork?

* Balanced — you work comfortably in both modes.

From *Games Teams Play,* by Leslie Bendaly. © McGraw-Hill Ryerson 1996

7.5 FLYING HIGH ✪ ✪

Objectives

To increase team members' awareness of the unique contributions different team members make.

To increase individual team members' awareness of the importance of their contribution to team performance.

To increase individuals' sense of responsibility for the successful completion of team tasks.

Materials Required

Provided: Handout
Other: Scissors, construction paper, glue and/or tape

Steps

1. Divide the team into subgroups of preferably four or more members in each group.

2. Provide each group with scissors, several sheets of construction paper, fast setting glue, and/or tape.

3. Give the following instructions:

   Each group's goal is to develop the best paper airplane that has ever been flown.

   You will be given 15 minutes to make and test fly your paper airplanes.

   After the 15-minute mark we will test each plane against the others to see which can fly the farthest.

4. Once the winning design team has been declared, distribute copies of the "Team Members' Contribution Worksheet"

(Handout 7.5.1). Ask the groups to use this worksheet to help them consider the role played or contribution made by each team member to the design, construction, and testing of their plane. Ask them to be prepared to share at least one contribution made by each team member. Time required for this step depends on size of groups and level of discussion. Average time required: 15 minutes.

Discussion Questions

1) What did you learn from this activity?

Common responses:
I recognized that:

- team members make contributions that often go unnoticed.

- what appear to be small contributions can make a big difference.

- each member brings different strengths to a team task.

2) How can we use this learning to strengthen the team?

Common response:
Responses will vary depending on team needs. They could include:

- We need to better consider members' strengths when assigning tasks.

- We need to remember to tap team members' skills that may be less obvious.

  If the discussion leads to the development of specific commitments to action, recap the commitments, and check for consensus.

Outcome

Heightened awareness of the different strengths members bring to the team.

A recognition of the need to better tap team members' skills and talents.

A list of commitments to action that will result in better use of team members' capabilities.

Team Members' Contribution

PARTICIPANT'S WORKSHEET — GROUP

Allotted time: 15 minutes

As a group list the contributions each team member made in the design, construction, and test flight of your paper airplane. The following questions are meant to stimulate your thinking, but do not limit yourself to the possible contributions listed.

Which members   – took leadership roles?
                        – participated most actively?
                        – influenced decisions most strongly?
                        – brought particular skills or experience to the task?
                        – were most creative?
                        – displayed enthusiasm?
                        – motivated others?

Team Member's Name	Contribution(s)

From *Games Teams Play*, by Leslie Bendaly. © McGraw-Hill Ryerson 1996

7.6 ORGANIZATIONAL TRIVIA ✪ ✪

Objectives

To increase team members' common knowledge of the organization.

To increase pride in the organization.

Time Required: 20 minutes +

Background

At one time teams could get by with being familiar with only their immediate work environment: their own department, unit, or their own project. As organizational walls collapsed and it became evident that every team is part of a system,* the realization that team members must be well informed about their organization as a whole became clear.

This game emphasizes the need to be organizationally aware and tests and increases team members' organizational knowledge. It is also meant to be fun.

Materials Required

Provided: Handout, Organizational Trivia Cards, Score Cards
Other: Set of answers, pens/pencils

Steps

Note: It is easy to develop many variations of the following game using the organizational trivia cards.

Pre Workshop

- Read the Organizational Trivia workout guidelines.

- Select organizational trivia cards that you believe best apply to your organi-

---

* In a system each part is affected by every other part and affects every other part.

zation. You require at least eight cards as the team must draw eight. Having more than eight increases the interest and adds an element of chance. You may develop your own questions using the blank cards provided.

- You must prepare answers to each question. Put each answer on a piece of paper, fold it, and put the number that corresponds to the question on the outside.

- You require one set of cards and answers for each group.

1. Distribute the Organizational Trivia workout guidelines (Handout 7.6.1), organizational trivia cards, answers, and score cards.

2. Review the rules.

3. Break into subgroups of four or more members.

4. Compare the scores and declare the winner.

5. Debriefing is optional. This workout can stand on its own.

Discussion Questions

1) How does the team's level of organizational knowledge affect it?

2) What might the team do to help ensure it keeps tuned into the larger organizational picture?

Outcome

Increased awareness of personal levels of organizational knowledge.

Recognition of the importance of keeping informed about the larger organizational picture.

Increased organizational knowledge.

Commitment to staying in tune with the larger organizational picture.

Organizational Trivia

WORKOUT GUIDELINES — GROUP

The leader will ask the organizational trivia questions and give the answers. The role of the leader rotates after two questions.

Questions are on the organizational trivia cards. The answer to each question can be found on the folded slip of paper with the corresponding number.

Each team will answer eight questions.

Steps

1. Any team member pulls an organizational trivia card without looking and hands it to the leader.

2. The leader reads the question.

3. The group confers and must agree on an answer.

4. The group has two chances to give the correct response.

5. The leader gives the correct answer.

6. The leader records the score.

The steps above are repeated for the additional seven cards.

Scoring

If team answers correctly first time, score 20 points.

If team answers correctly second time, score 10 points.

If team does not get the answer, score 0 points.

From *Games Teams Play*, by Leslie Bendaly. © McGraw-Hill Ryerson 1996

1. Give the year your company/ organization was established.

2. List two stated organizational values.

3. State your company's mission statement.

4. State your company's/ organization's philosophy statement.

WORKOUT 7.6: Organizational Trivia Cards

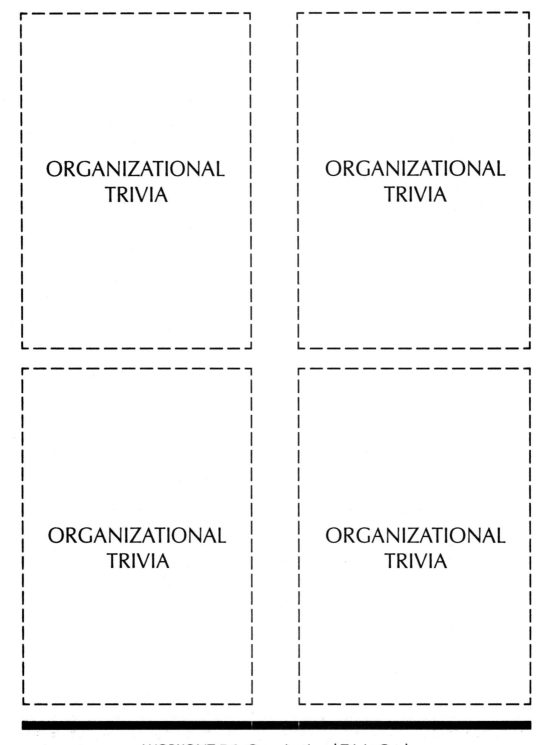

ORGANIZATIONAL TRIVIA

ORGANIZATIONAL TRIVIA

ORGANIZATIONAL TRIVIA

ORGANIZATIONAL TRIVIA

WORKOUT 7.6: Organizational Trivia Cards

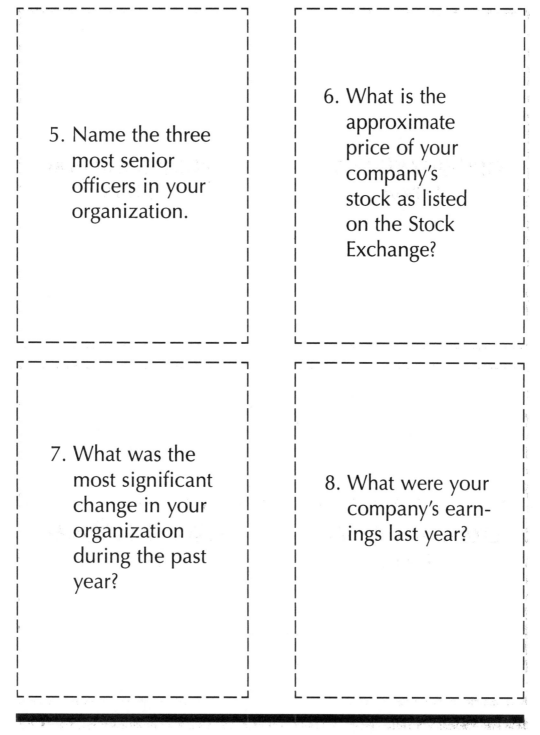

5. Name the three most senior officers in your organization.

6. What is the approximate price of your company's stock as listed on the Stock Exchange?

7. What was the most significant change in your organization during the past year?

8. What were your company's earnings last year?

WORKOUT 7.6: Organizational Trivia Cards

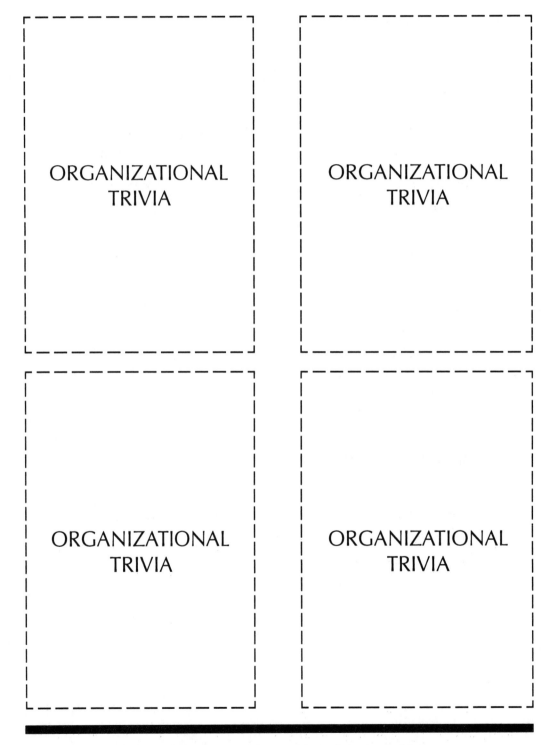

ORGANIZATIONAL
TRIVIA

ORGANIZATIONAL
TRIVIA

ORGANIZATIONAL
TRIVIA

ORGANIZATIONAL
TRIVIA

WORKOUT 7.6: Organizational Trivia Cards

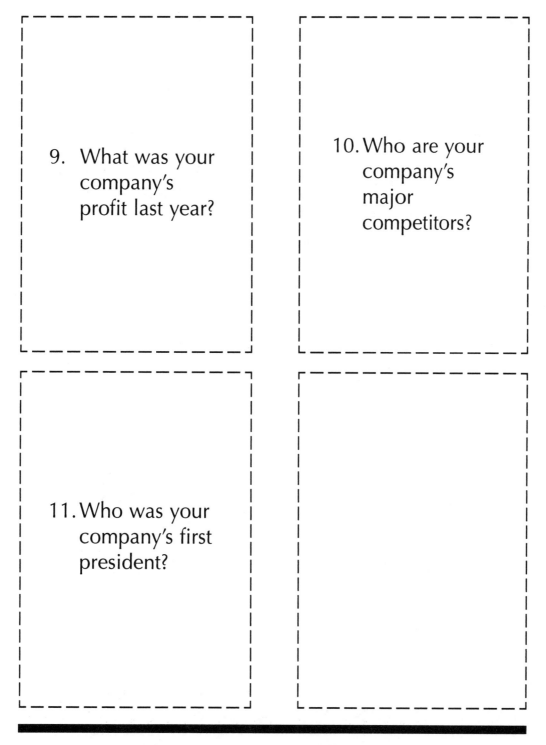

9. What was your
   company's
   profit last year?

10. Who are your
    company's
    major
    competitors?

11. Who was your
    company's first
    president?

WORKOUT 7.6: Organizational Trivia Cards

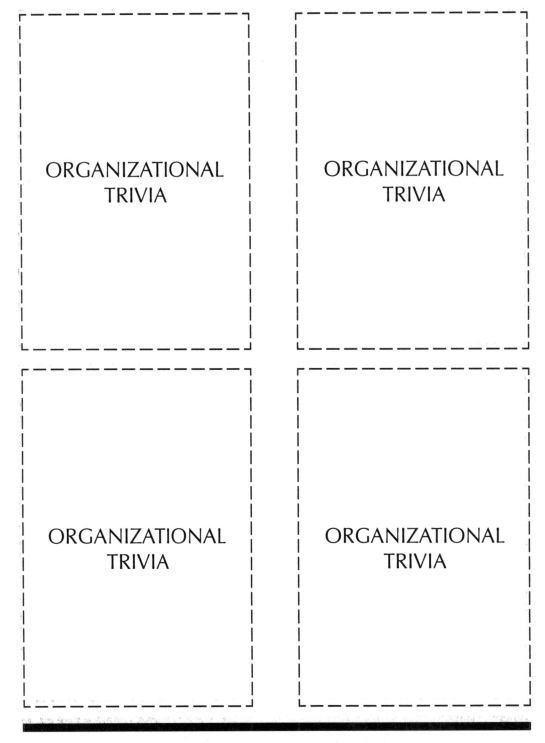

ORGANIZATIONAL
TRIVIA

ORGANIZATIONAL
TRIVIA

ORGANIZATIONAL
TRIVIA

ORGANIZATIONAL
TRIVIA

WORKOUT 7.6: Organizational Trivia Cards

From *Games Teams Play*, by Leslie Bendaly. © McGraw-Hill Ryerson 1996

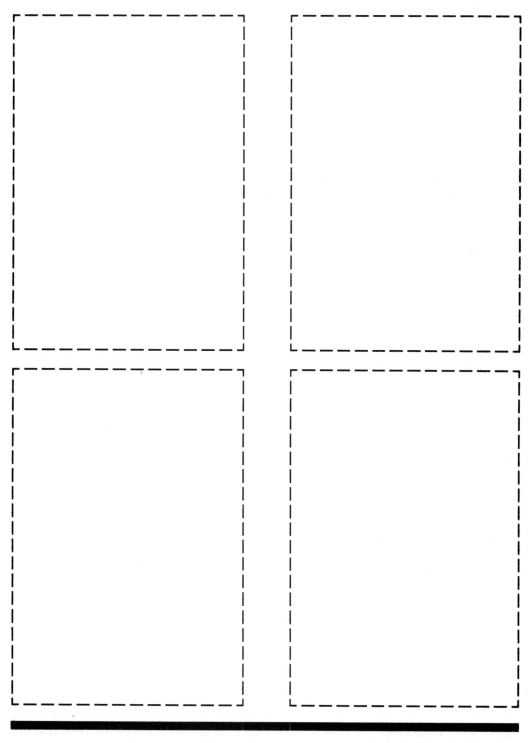

WORKOUT 7.6: Organizational Trivia Cards

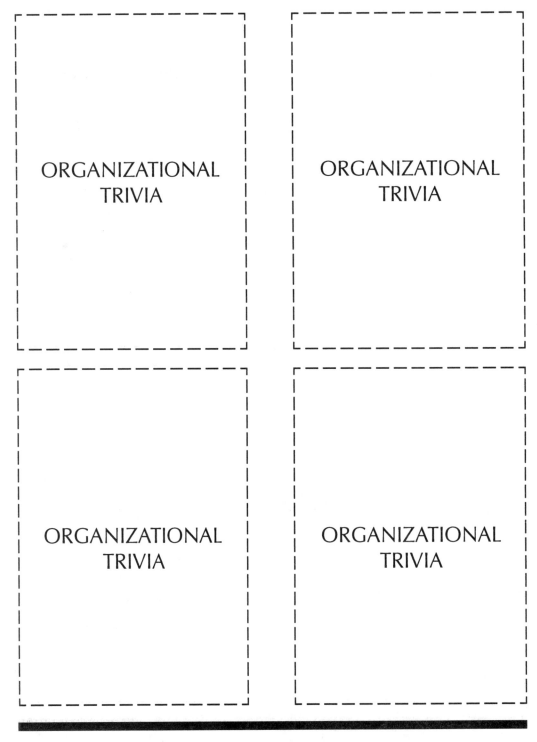

ORGANIZATIONAL
TRIVIA

ORGANIZATIONAL
TRIVIA

ORGANIZATIONAL
TRIVIA

ORGANIZATIONAL
TRIVIA

WORKOUT 7.6: Organizational Trivia Cards

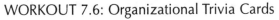

Question	Score		
1	20	10	0
2	20	10	0
3	20	10	0
4	20	10	0
5	20	10	0
6	20	10	0
7	20	10	0
8	20	10	0
Total			

Question	Score		
1	20	10	0
2	20	10	0
3	20	10	0
4	20	10	0
5	20	10	0
6	20	10	0
7	20	10	0
8	20	10	0
Total			

Question	Score		
1	20	10	0
2	20	10	0
3	20	10	0
4	20	10	0
5	20	10	0
6	20	10	0
7	20	10	0
8	20	10	0
Total			

Question	Score		
1	20	10	0
2	20	10	0
3	20	10	0
4	20	10	0
5	20	10	0
6	20	10	0
7	20	10	0
8	20	10	0
Total			

WORKOUT 7.6: Score Cards

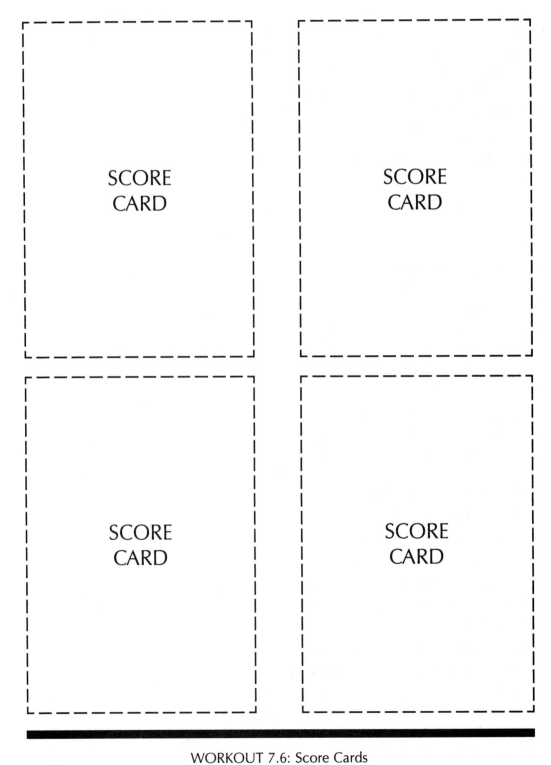

WORKOUT 7.6: Score Cards

From *Games Teams Play*, by Leslie Bendaly. © McGraw-Hill Ryerson 1996

7.7 PERSONAL SPOT CHECK
✪ ✪

Objectives
To increase team members' awareness of the importance of their day-to-day behaviors, attitudes, and contributions to the success of the team.

To challenge team members to examine their strengths and opportunities for growth.

To strengthen team members' contribution to the team.

Time Required: 45 minutes +

Background
High performance teams are greater than the sum of their parts. However, for a team to reach its potential, each part must be contributing at its full potential.

Team members often get so busy with the job they are there to do that they overlook their team responsibilities. Most people want and tend to be good team members — they just forget at times. Simply jogging their memories can make a great difference to teamwork effectiveness.

The checklist provided in this workout reminds team members of their team responsibilities and gives them an opportunity to engage in self-assessment.

For groups that have never discussed team members' responsibilities, and what are and what are not realistic expectations, the following questions can stimulate important discussion. As the issues raised could be of a sensitive nature, care should be taken to ensure discussion is well facilitated.

Materials Required

Provided: Handout

Steps

1. Introduce the workout with a brief discussion of the importance of each member's contribution.

2. Distribute copies of the Self-Assessment participant's worksheet "Weighing Your Contribution" (Handout 7.7.1). Allow approximately ten minutes for its completion.

   Note: If the team is sufficiently well developed to allow for honest feedback go to step 3. If not, skip to step 4.

3. Ask participants to work in groups of two or three, share the results of their "Weighing Your Contribution" assessment, and give one another feedback on each statement as follows:

   a) Yes, I see you as you see yourself.

   b) I think you underestimate yourself here. For example . . .

   c) In this area, my experience is that you . . . (positive examples). I think you could make an even greater contribution to the team in this area if you . . .

   Allow 15–20 minutes

   Note: In highly developed teams there is no need to break into smaller groups if the team is a manageable size for this workout. The whole team can effectively provide team members with valuable feedback.

4. Ask each team member to identify and share with the team at least one posi-

tive contribution he or she makes to the team and one commitment to action for personal improvement.

Tip: Ask members to make note of their personal commitments to action and be prepared to either comment on their progress at a team meeting within the next month or to ask for input from team members as to whether change in their behavior is evident.

Outcome

Increased personal responsibility for performance.

Strengthened individual performance.

Your Notes

Weighing Your Contribution

PARTICIPANT'S WORKSHEET

Please rate each of the following statements according to the consistency with which you believe it applies to you

- — 1 never
- — 2 occasionally
- — 3 usually
- — 4 always

If selecting a 3 or 4 rating, give example under "Evidence".

1. I participate fully in team meetings.   **1   2   3   4**

Evidence:

_____

_____

2. I demonstrate a positive attitude.   **1   2   3   4**

Evidence:

_____

_____

3. If I have concern with something someone **1   2   3   4**
   has said or done I go directly to that person
   (rather than talking to others about them).

Evidence:

_____

_____

HANDOUT 7.7.1

From *Games Teams Play*, by Leslie Bendaly. © McGraw-Hill Ryerson 1996

Self-Assessment — Weighing Your Contribution (cont'd)

4. I listen openly to others' ideas.   **1   2   3   4**

Evidence:

_____

_____

5. I sincerely celebrate others' successes.   **1   2   3   4**

Evidence:

_____

_____

6. I follow through on anything I agree to do.   **1   2   3   4**

Evidence:

_____

_____

7. I represent my team positively to non-team   **1   2   3   4**
   members.

Evidence:

_____

_____

8. I willingly share the load.   **1   2   3   4**

Evidence:

_____

_____

HANDOUT 7.7.1

Self-Assessment — Weighing Your Contribution (cont'd)

9. If the facts are not clear, I check for clarification rather than making assumptions. **1 2 3 4**

Evidence:

_____

_____

10. I look for opportunities to make others stars. **1 2 3 4**

Evidence:

_____

_____

11. I meet deadlines. **1 2 3 4**

Evidence:

_____

_____

12. I take the initiative to do whatever needs to be done. **1 2 3 4**

Evidence:

_____

_____

For statements that do not consistently describe you, ask yourself—Is this something I should do more of? If so, make a personal commitment to action for the item.

Note: A commitment to action is a specific action you might take / something you will do differently in future.

HANDOUT 7.7.1

From *Games Teams Play*, by Leslie Bendaly. © McGraw-Hill Ryerson 1996

7.8 A TALENT HUNT ✪

Objectives

To identify and recognize the skills and abilities of each team member.

To ensure team members' skills and abilities are tapped by the team.

To show appreciation for the strengths members bring to the team.

Your Notes

Time Required: 45 minutes

Background

Too frequently teams tap only a small percentage of what team members have to offer; only the basic skills required to fulfil the team member's job description are used. High performance team members know one another's strengths, look for opportunities to use those strengths, and celebrate them.

Materials Required

Other: Large colored sheets of paper or light Bristol board, felt markers

Steps

1. Ask team members to jot down each team member's name and under each name develop a list of his or her skills, abilities, and talents. Emphasize the importance of including talents that the members may not use on a daily basis at work.

2. Post large colored sheets of paper, one for each team member, around the room. Place a felt marker by each paper.

3. Ask team members to take the lists they have developed and transfer the talents

they have identified to the large colored sheets.

4. As a group examine the lists and ensure each strength on each list is mentioned. Do this with energy — this is a mini-celebration of team members' contributions. Ask the member whose talents are being discussed if any of their talents have been missed. If so, add them. For each list identify:

   a) the talents the team is fully tapping;

   b) the talents the team isn't fully tapping.

5. Select at least one talent that isn't being fully tapped for each team member and ask the group, "How could the team better use this talent?"

6. Ask the team to develop recommendations as to how they can keep team members' talents in front of the team and better use them on an ongoing basis.

7. Recap and check for consensus on any recommendations for action.

   Tip: Give members their own sheets of talents to take with them. Suggest they post their sheets or a smaller version of them, to remind themselves to fully utilize their talents.

Outcome

Greater awareness of personal abilities.

Greater use of team members' skills.

Greater sense of team.

Increased personal pride.

7.9 AS OTHERS SEE US ✪

Objectives

To challenge team members to:

(1) Reflect on their personal style.

(2) Make commitments to strengthening their personal contribution to the team.

Background:

Growth happens when individuals pause to reflect on their performance or behavior, identify strengths and opportunities for growth, and act on these opportunities.

Materials

Provided: Handout

Steps

1. Distribute two copies of the participant's worksheet "As Others See Us" (Handout 7.9.1) to each member.

2. Ask team members to work in teams of two to complete two copies of page 1 of the worksheet, as instructed.

3. Allow approximately 25 minutes for the partners to complete the worksheets and discuss it amongst themselves. (If there are particular issues that are likely to be brought out in the discussion, more time may be required.)

4. Ask each team member to share a characteristic that he or she and his or her partner sees as a strength, plus one opportunity for growth.

   Tip: It works well to have the partner talk about strengths the other brings to the team, and the team member iden-

Your Notes

tify his or her own opportunities for personal growth.

Outcome

Heightened awareness of personal style and characteristics.

Commitment to personal development.

As Others See Us

PARTICIPANT'S WORKSHEET

Consider the characteristics below and put an X beside those that best describe you.

— Cooperative

— Informed

— Participative

— Organized

— Trustworthy

— Positive (approach issues constructively)

— Negative (tend to look for the problems not the solutions)

— Open and honest

— Aggressive

— Assertive

— A natural leader

— Easy to deal with

— Often involved in conflict

— The one who resolves conflict

— See others' points of view

— Willing to compromise

— Cope well with change

— Follow through on commitments

— Fun to be with

— Examine issues objectively

— Resistant to change

— Judge quickly

— Highly skilled in job/profession

— High personal work standards

— Can be depended on

— Reluctant to move from own position or point of view

— Make others feel good about themselves

— Flexible

HANDOUT 7.9.1

Consider the same characteristics and put an X beside those that best describe your partner.

Name of your partner: _____

— Cooperative

— Informed

— Participative

— Organized

— Trustworthy

— Positive (approach issues constructively)

— Negative (tend to look for the problems not the solutions)

— Open and honest

— Aggressive

— Assertive

— A natural leader

— Easy to deal with

— Often involved in conflict

— The one who resolves conflict

— Sees others' points of view

— Willing to compromise

— Copes well with change

— Follows through on commitments

— Fun to be with

— Examines issues objectively

— Resistant to change

— Judges quickly

— Highly skilled in job/profession

— High personal work standards

— Can be depended on

— Reluctant to move from own position or point of view

— Makes others feel good about themselves

— Flexible

Discussion Outcomes

List two strengths you bring to the team.

_____

_____

List any opportunities for personal growth.

_____

_____

HANDOUT 7.9.1

From *Games Teams Play*, by Leslie Bendaly. © McGraw-Hill Ryerson 1996

ABOUT THE AUTHOR

Leslie Bendaly is a leading specialist in organizational change and teamwork. Much in demand as a speaker and trainer, her audiences and clients reflect all sectors of the economy from Fortune 500 companies to government and health care organizations. A small sample of her clients includes IBM, CIBC, Aetna Canada, Air Canada, Bell Canada, GE Capital Technologies and Sun Life.

Leslie is president of Ortran Associates Inc., a Toronto-based consulting firm.

Leslie receives wide exposure. She is a member of the MICA seminar faculty as their teamwork specialist, as well as seminar leader for the Ontario Hospital Association. She has published articles on teamwork and change, is interviewed on radio and television, and is quoted in business publications such as *The Globe and Mail*. Her work is showcased in videos, and she is manager and editor of *Teamwork Essentials*, a report for team-based organizations.

Her book on teamwork, *Strength in Numbers* (McGraw-Hill Ryerson), has become a top seller and has been chosen by many organizations as a handbook for their managers and teams. Leslie's work has been recognized in *Who's Who in Canadian Business*.

Products and Services
Provided by Leslie Bendaly and Ortran

- Workshops

- Keynote Addresses

  Contact: Virginia Mantycki
  Phone: (416) 440-0532
  Fax: (416) 489-1173

- *Teamwork Essentials.* The newsletter that provides you and your teams with tips, tools and information that can be immediately used to accelerate their development. It's reproducible!

  Contact: Ortran Associates
  Phone: (416) 440-0532
  Fax: (416) 489-1173

- Trainer Certification. Certify your trainers to lead our team learning workshop "Creating Teams That Work".

  Contact: Mica Management
           Resources
  Attention: Ms. Krista Beaudry
  Phone: (416) 366-6422
  Fax: (416) 362-6422

- *Strength in Numbers: Turning Work Groups into Teams* by Leslie Bendaly, published by McGraw-Hill Ryerson.
  ISBN 0-07-551023-5
  $17.95 (Cdn.)

- *Games Teams Play.* Trainers looseleaf version also available, published by McGraw-Hill Ryerson.
  ISBN 0-07-552719-7
  $120.00 (Cdn.)

  Contact: McGraw-Hill Ryerson
  Phone: (905) 430-5000
  Toronto toll-free number:
          (905) 428-2222